SINO-PAK RELATIONS: STRATEGIC AND ECONOMIC DIMENSIONS AND THEIR IMPLICATIONS ON INDIA

GAURAV SUBBA

*This book is dedicated to My wife Mrs. Prabesika
Pradhan,*

my respected Mother in law and father in law

and also to my respected Father and mother

and

my dear daughter Gaursika Cherungma Subba.

Contents

About The Author

Mr. GAURAV SUBBA (MANGYUNG)

Gaurav Subba is a dedicated independent research scholar with expertise in international relations and governance. He has actively contributed to academia and public discourse through his extensive research and publications.

Educational Qualifications
Gaurav holds an impressive academic background:
- *Bachelor of Arts (General) (B.A.G)*
- *Bachelor of Education (B.Ed)*
- *Master of Arts in International Relations/Politics (M.A.)*
- *Master of Philosophy (M.Phil) in International Relations/ Politics*

Professional Experience
Gaurav's professional journey includes:
1. Assistant Lecturer: Taught at Salesian College, Siliguri,

West Bengal, in 2016.
2. Entrepreneur: Managed "Gaurav Corner," offering digital services, stationery, old-age pension facilitation, and customer service support.

3. Currently working as an Assistant Sub-Inspector under Urban Development Department, Government of Sikkim, Soreng District.

Participation in Seminars and Workshops
He has participated in numerous national and international conferences e-seminars/conferences, showcasing his dedication to academic growth and global discussions:
• *Attended the National Security Seminar on "From Contest to Cooperation: A Vision for Shared Prosperity in the Indo-Pacific Region" (Nov 2–3, 2017) organized by the United Service Institution of India, New Delhi.*
• *Participated in a seminar at the Institute of Chinese Studies at the India*
International Centre on "The Age of Uncertainty," delivered by Michael Krepon (Aug 9, 2017).
• *Engaged in the Workshop on Global Studies at the MMAJ Academy of*
International Studies, Jamia Millia Islamia (March 6–7, 2018).
• *Attended the Indo-Pacific Regional Dialogue organized by the National Maritime*
Foundation at Manekshaw Centre, New Delhi (Feb 27, 2018).

Publications
Gaurav has made significant contributions as an author:
Books
1. Global and Local Context of Good Governance: A Study

of Sikkim
2. Understanding Ethnic Harmony in Sikkim
3. Penned

Research Articles
- *"Sino-Pak Axis and Its Implications on India" – Published in IJRAR, May 2021 (Vol. 8, Issue 2).*
- *"Perspective of India towards Sino-Pak Collaboration" – Published in Natural Volatiles & Essential Oils, 2021 (Vol. 8, Issue 4).*

Contact Information
- *Phone: +91 9002687111*
- *Email: gauravsubba28@gmail.com*

Foreword

Mrs. Prabesika Pradhan

In an era where global power dynamics are increasingly influenced by regional partnerships, understanding the complexities of international relations has never been more critical. The strategic and economic partnership between China and Pakistan is one such alliance that continues to shape the geopolitical and security landscape of South Asia. This book, Sino-Pak Relations: Strategic and Economic Dimensions and Their Implications on India, provides an in-depth analysis of this evolving partnership and its ramifications for India and the region as a whole.

Through meticulous research and theoretical grounding, the author delves into the historical foundations of the Sino-Pak alliance, its strategic depth, and its economic underpinnings, such as the transformative China-Pakistan Economic Corridor. Equally significant is the examination of how this bilateral relationship intersects with India's geopolitical aspirations and challenges. The triangulation of interests among China, Pakistan, and India makes this study a timely and essential contribution to the field of international relations.

This book stands out for its balanced approach to complex issues. It not only sheds light on the economic and military dimensions of the Sino-Pak alliance but also offers insightful perspectives on the broader implications of this relationship on regional stability, security, and economic development. By situating the analysis within the frameworks of international relations theories and securitization, the author enables readers to grasp the deeper strategic calculations driving this partnership.

For scholars, policymakers, and professionals seeking to navigate the intricate power play in South Asia, this work provides both context and clarity. It invites readers to critically engage with questions of strategy, cooperation, and competition in one of the world's most dynamic and contested regions.

I commend the author for their dedication to this important research and for offering a resource that will undoubtedly become a cornerstone for further discussions on South Asian geopolitics.

[Mrs. Prabesika Pradhan]

[Independent Research Scholar]

[25/12/2024]

Preface

The global landscape of power dynamics is continuously reshaped by geopolitical alliances, and the Sino- Pak axis stands out as a pivotal partnership that has significantly influenced regional and global geopolitics. This examines the intricate dimensions of the China-Pakistan alliance, analyzing its historical evolution, strategic imperatives, and far-reaching implications for regional stability, with a specific focus on its impact on India.

The origins of the Sino-Pak axis can be traced to shared strategic objectives and mutual interests, which have transcended ideological differences and fluctuating domestic contexts. The partnership has matured into a multifaceted collaboration encompassing military, economic, and political spheres, epitomized by landmark initiatives like the China-Pakistan Economic Corridor (CPEC). These developments not only redefine bilateral ties but also reshape regional power equations.

This work seeks to provide a comprehensive understanding of the axis, delving into its historical context, key areas of cooperation,and the broader implications for India's strategic landscape. By drawing on theories of international relations, security studies, and the concept of techno-politics, it presents an analytical framework to explore how this alliance challenges traditional power balances and influences policymaking in South Asia.

The study also sheds lighting the complex triangular relationship between China, Pakistan, and India, highlighting the enduring challenges and opportunities for peace and cooperation in the region. At its core, this book aims to offer insights into how the Sino-Pak axis has not only transformed regional dynamics but also serves as a critical case study for understanding contemporary geopolitics.

This is the culmination of extensive research and aims to contribute to the discourse on international relations and strategic studies. I hope it provides readers with a nuanced perspective on the intricacies of this crucial alliance and fosters a deeper appreciation of the geopolitical forces shaping our world today.

Gaurav Subba

16/12/2024

Acknowledgements

I would like to take this opportunity for My Deepest and sincere gratitude and thankfullness to respected Prof. (Dr.) Sukhwant S. Bindra " Director Research Amity Institute of International Studies (AIIS) & Amity Institute of Public Policy (AIPP), Noida, Uttar Pradesh. & respected Prof. (Dr.) Nagalaxmi M Raman "Director & Head Amity Institute of International Studies (AIIS) Noida, Uttar Pradesh.

Also i would like to thank (Amity University, Noida, Uttar Pradesh), and Amity University Library and E-Library, Online Magazines, E-Journals, E-Newspaper, Google Scholar, Indian Council of World Affairs (ICWA), E-book/websites, Indian Think Thanks, & AI off course.

Also never to forget faculties, staffs, friends and families. I beg pardon for if i have missed any/one to acknowledge.

Sincerely,

Gaurav Subba.

24th December 2024

CHAPTER I

Introduction

1.1 Introduction

There are essentially three forms of relationships between people, organizations and nations. Threat relationships, exchange integrative and relations relationships exist. There are threats relations[1]. Threats are first used to track the condition of another person when products and services are provided in exchange for goods and services in the second form of agreement. In order to achieve one another's interests as well as to promote one's 'national interest,' the Integrative Elaboration parties show a good sense of solidarity, utilizing economic and military trade and helping. In a number of ways, the third party relationship between Pakistan and China is special and comparable in the annals of contemporary international relations. The Sino Pakistani relations in the past five decades symbolize stability and development in the maze of foreign affairs, though intrinsically asymmetry in a power base, cultural perspectives and a divergent socio-policy sense exists. Despite the numerous changes in national governments and in various external contexts, the relationship has survived and prospered. During this era, China-Pakistan ties advanced from 'right,' 'friendly,' 'friendly' and a special relationship or cordiality. In the age of domestic fluctuations and instability and political upheavals that foreign affairs were unable to avoid, Pakistan was one of only two nations with a predictable ties to Beijing, with one North Korea being the other. In the Sino-Pak ties, aside from tolerant alternative political and military law periods in Pakistan, there have been a number of upheavals and disruptions of foreign policy transitions since Mao. The Cultural Revolution in China Its ties have, over the years, not only taken into account political and military sectors but also other sectors including finance, foreign policy, research and technology, information exchange, manufacturing, logistics and, above all, nuclear fields.

In order to be the primary determinants of ties between States, religious issues are substituted for security interest and real political factors, the establishment of the Unique Partnership between Pakistan and China is more strategically evaluated.

This analysis of Sino Pakistani ties is focused on the premise that countries interact with their ideology or social structures rather than with their countries as such. In other terms, ideology is not the main determinant of international politics, and alliances or enmities between nations are created not through intellectual affinities or inconsistencies but by dictates of national interests.

Pakistan's ties with China are focused on mutual concepts of non-interference. Eastern Pakistan and Xinxiang are instances of such non-interference. In 1949, Pakistan acknowledged China. She refused to assist the secessionists of East Pakistan and backed the unity and territorial integrity of Pakistan. The 1962 Chinese-Indian war reinforced these ties even further[2]. India had implications on China's affairs in Pakistan in the period of Indo-Pakistan. India has made its strategic ally to the US in combating Sino-Pakistan ties. Both countries' foreign policy (Pakistan and China) reveals each other's desires. China's presence in Pakistan promotes Pakistan's economy, and China's trading path from Pakistan around the world is secure and secure[3]. China is using Pakistan as a portal to its export, constructing infrastructure such as China Pakistan's CPEC, to facilitate access between Xinjiang and the Indian Ocean. China is building its infrastructure China also gets significant political support from Pakistan, especially in forums such as the Islamic Conference Organization (OIC). The Chinese trade is permanently under pressure from Pakistan's turmoil. China, however, has a shorter commercial path via the port of Gwadar. The big infrastructure in Pakistan is being built by China for CPEC, for example. The main aim is to expand Chinese exports of products not only in Pakistan but worldwide[4]. These ties would be stronger and longer lasting if Pakistan were willing to oppose extremism and insurgency. Since China often criticises Pakistani Taliban practices in China's Xinxiang province. It would be a huge challenge to Pakistan's brilliant future if it could not meet them. As opposed to the West, China is seen as Pakistan's — all-weather mate. Chinese apprehensions of Uighurs, not India, underpin today's security collaboration with Pakistan. A multi-faceted curriculum needs to be established to familiarize each other with the society, language, activities and background of the two states. In the shadow of instability, Sino-Indian ties are constrained by the ensuing problems which reveal friction for the two countries.

China is a vast country. Through eighteen nations, China has territorial and boundary issues. The exception is Pakistan's Islamic Republic which maintains its salary. The following countries with territorial and borders on China are listed: Japan, South Korea, Bhutan, Taiwan, Kazakhstan, Laos, Brunei, Tajikistan, Cambodia, Kyrgyzstan, Malaysia, Mongolia, Afghanistan, Japan, Vietnam, North Korea, Northern India, Nepal[5].

China-Pakistan ties are another repercussion for India. There is mutual trust and friendship, and China and Pakistan are "all weather mates." There have been near friendly ties between them. Over time and distance these relationships have been checked. Almost without changing domestic developments, their working relationship was reinforced and vigorous, despite drastic changes at international and regional levels. Since friendship is based on reverence for UN Charter ideals and the five principles of peaceful coexistence[6]. It shares faith and trust and is fostered and enriched by high-level daily connections. Both sides are shared in the fostering of stability and development in South Asia and partner with them. They reject transnational and racial nationalism and aspire to achieve a just international political and economic imperative. China and Pakistan also cooperate on their issues and engage in international and regional meetings. We still hope to see continued prosperity and strengthening of ties between the two countries, especially in the coming period[7].

China-Pakistan decided to construct an energy and financial corridor, called China Pakistan Economic Corridor, during the Musharraf period (CPEC). Kashgar connected the south-western Pakistan port of Gwadar in China's Xinjiang Uygur Province (Baluchistan). In the broader sense of China's regional and large-script initiative, called the "one belt, one road to policy," the CPEC will be crucial for India[8]. India protested the corridor by passing across Pakistan's contested Azad Kashmir region. It is also correct that certain very important territorial controversies surrounding China, India and Pakistan also have to be settled. If, though, it is imaginative, the planned CPEC would open up a new panorama of regional economic cooperation and stability[9].

In response to the project Gwadar Kashgar, the changing regional climate offers the Indian policymakers many choices. First of all, India may continue to object to and to hold demonstrations that may hinder or block the building of the corridor (CPEC). Secondly, India might take a more constructive corridor strategy by touching Pakistan and China in order to have trilateral cooperation in the proposed building. There are already separate relations between India and Pakistan. Last but not least, trilateral cooperation (China-India-Pakistan) would initiate regional economic cooperation, regional inclusion and human capital development. If it happens, the real economic arteries transforming the world are China and South Asia.[10].

By implementing the policies of "influence sphere" (Levine) and "perl string," China will expand its influence in India[11]. The encircling strategy of India by China is responding to by the development of ties with Taiwan, Japan, Vietnam etc. in New Delhi, looking at east policy. Both countries are entitled to be recognised as regional and local forces because of their enormous economic development. Both states battle for the equalisation of the strategic game, but they're in a multiple game[12]. In the context of India, this will tremendously develop the probability of reaching Afghanistan, improving the vast flea market in central Asia and providing access to the excessive natural wealth of the area, which India had dreamed of. Pakistan will have huge advantages in this regard as well. The antagonism towards India will also be stopped[13].

There are also global objectives for China and India. China has been less arguing and follows close diplomacy and India is clearly committed to playing a global position. In the United Nations Security Council, India and Japan requested veto power status (UNSC). To date, China has not bolstered India's attempts to become a permanent member of the UN Security Council and the nuclear supplier group (NSG). However, by setting up a five-plus Community of five permanent representatives India has ensured that the UN strengthens its crucial role in the UNSC.

1.1.1 Foundations of the China-Pakistan Friendly Alliance

China-Pakistan entente cordiale has undergone its crux and mutual support in the every hour of need[14].

1. Diplomatic aid

Pakistan has always provided the People's Republic of China with a critical source of diplomatic assistance in times of need, whether the defense of the Chinese interests in Tibet, Taiwan or China's Xinjiang zone. Pakistan's political support for China is also compounded by the pace of its pioneering visit to Beijing in 1972[15]. In Pakistan, China had to open up the global phase.

Recognizing the Pakistani Democratic Republic, Chinese Premier Wen Jiabao talked to the parliament in Pakistan: "We got useful support from Pakistan at the critical times when China pursued the breaking of external blockades, the restoration of its legitimate seat at the United Nations, and the normalisation of ties with the US. We received clear and absolute assistance from Pakistan on these important issues relating to Taiwan, Tibet and Xinjiang"[16] .

2. Corridor approaching Energy

In the quest for energy resources for the expanding economy of Pakistan, strategic links with Europe and central Asian states have been crucial for China. It is the power strip of Islamabad that seeks to repay the lasting friendship of China. As a first move towards an extended energy corridor scheme for Gwadar to China, Pakistan strengthened the harbour of Gwadar in 2006. In the next 20 years, Pakistan will be generating a transit fee of EUR 60 billion a year and China will guard the critical energy route[17] . Now, after the United States, China is the second largest oil consumer in the world. By 2025, its intake can be predicted to be doubled. Single supply rivals are India and China. For China's regional power proposal, Pakistan is vital. By reducing billions of dollars from Sudan into Iran and extending replacement transport routes across Pakistan, Bangladesh and Thailand and Myanmar, China is disseminating its oil sources[18] (Kumar, 2007).

3. Strategic Partnership

The strategic partnership between Pakistan and China is a continuous assurance for win-win. The establishment in China and Pakistan is neutral in achieving specific objectives by thoroughly using the power of the capital on either side. The relationship between China and Pakistan is based on integrity, optimism, common goals and recognition of the opportunities and values of one another. Hu Jintao suggested a "strategic alliance" with Pakistan to improve and deepen bilateral ties when Musharraf visited China in April 2006[19]. The scheme stated the importance of China as a strategic partner for Pakistan. Surprisingly, this conglomerate does not achieve its greatest ability. In this regard, Chinese Prime Minister Wen Jiabao said during his December 2010 visit to Islamabad that the foreign and regional circumstances are still complicated. China and Pakistan, as all-weather strategic allies, can communicate and collaborate together, as well as face threats together... China-Pakistan pragmatic collaboration is an important component of the bilateral strategic relationship, with positive prospects. China hopes to collaborate with Pakistan to provide more opportunities to its population[20].

4. Cooperation with Military

The connotation of Sino-Pakistan security relations is the eye of the tiger. They enhance the West's blame for Pakistan's expansion of nuclear arms. China has been Pakistan's main provider of weapons since 1965[21].

But the Chinese capitalises on Pakistan by trade undertakings, oil corridors, power plants and cables through unstable Northern parts of Pakistan. Reciprocal competition may be attributed to military cooperation between China and India. Following the India-US nuclear pact, China has agreed to take a step-by-step approach to Pakistan's long-term nuclear programme commitment. At the end of the visit of Prime Minister Wen Jiabao, in a joint press statement released in December 2010 both States — reiterated the fact that the values and spirit of the Friendship, Co-operation and Good Neighborly Treaty continue to enhance mutual confidence and co-operation in the military-security region. This leads the two countries and the country to achieve unity, safety and prosperity[22]. (Garver, 1996).

1.2 Statement of the Problem

The relationship between the countries in this ever changing and the interconnected world, forming an alliance as strategy to survive, develop, and rise as a powerful country becomes necessary. Therefore looking at the relationship between the China-Pakistan and the triangle relationship of China-Pakistan and India, this research study attempts to understand the Implications on India, focusing on major partnerships between China and Pakistan respectively. In a sub-continent where India and China is emerging as a powerful country and plays a significant role in shaping global politics, the relationship between India and China based on 'cooperation' and 'competition' makes it crucial to understand and study the factors causing implications on India by China-Pakistan axis.

India and China are two of the oldest civilisation nations in the world, once the biggest forces and today the populous counties. This is the two South Asian border regions with several overlapping interest groups, with historical explanations taking the shape of sharp gaps around the borders. Both countries are very active in the world economy and have nuclear capacity that can balance their rising aspirations with increasing military capability. In the light of Pakistan and India, on the other side, they share most of their geographical position as well as religious demographics. Moreover, several military and territorial tensions characterise bilateral ties between these two countries. The division of British India in 1947 formed two big, independent nations, India and Pakistan. The debris of India's division has clouded ties between Indo-Pak since 1947. About the fact that China and Pakistan's geographical position are driving them into a political and security relationship, there is still substantive collaboration between Pakistan and China, e.g. trading, boundary demarcation, air services and cultural agreements. Moreover, with the Innovative "New Silk Road" policy and providing financial and growth support to Pakistan, China is gradually growing its presence in the area. Nevertheless, India's contested boundaries with Pakistan and China continue creating instability through covert military collaboration between China and Pakistan by which Beijing has offered Pakistan's nuclear arms and missile programmes. The Sino-Pak axis therefore still gives India cause for alarm and obliges it to stay alert.

1.3 Research Questions

The broad question to be studied by this research study is:

With reference to China-Pakistan relationship,

1. What are the implications on India?
2. Why India is in this precarious position?
3. How India can transform itself through skillful strategy into a leading power?
4. What are the military ties between China and Pakistan?
5. What are the strategic ties between China and Pakistan?
6. What are the economic ties between China and Pakistan?

1.4 Importance of the Study

To put it very simply a state can grow to its fullest and have overall development only on companionship. On the other hand, seeing the rise and fall of tensions and disputes between the three countries i.e. China, India and Pakistan it can be said that the most immediate threat to any nation arises in its neighborhood and therefore this research study on Sino-Pak axis and its implications on India is very important and necessary to study and this deems fit. This study will also attempt to offer alternatives to maintain peace, stability and friendship, which is of utmost importance especially when these three have access to nuclear weapons.

1.5 Objectives of the Study

- To understand the implications on India caused by the Sino-Pak axis.
- To understand security ties between China and Pakistan.
- To understand the economic ties between China and Pakistan.
- To analyze strategic cooperation between China and Pakistan.
- To explore the alternatives and measures to mitigate the relationship of India-China-Pakistan.

1.6 Scope of the Study

The proposed study will only investigate the relationship between China, Pakistan and India. It will discuss the historical relations of these three countries and this study will restrict its focus only to military ties, economic ties, and strategic ties between China and Pakistan. Further it will try to explore the implications on India. It will not take into the considerations of the viewpoints of the other countries apart from India-China-Pakistan.

1.7 Research Methodology

For the proposed study, this study will be conducting a theoretical, descriptive and analytical type of research, with study of historical records and documents collected with assembling of contemporary significant data from the exclusive documents and accumulating database in order to comprehend the material and to arrive to a more complete understanding of "Sino-Pak axis and its implications on India", as well as, this study will carry on research relying upon qualitative approach, for which it will also take genuinely the up-to-date itineraries, references, interpretations, abstract-guides. The sources, which will be used, are both primary and secondary data. It will also use various publications by international bodies, books, magazines, journals, newspapers, reports, blogs, and websites, as well as the unpublished theses.

1.8 Literature Review

Although there are many works on the subject of Sino-Pak relations-by various authors, there has not been any major study on this particular subject, i.e. "Sino-Pak Relations: Strategic & Economic Dimensions", both these dimensions taken together. This is an area, which has remained generally under explored.

There are several other books on civil-military ties as well as the military's position as the most remarkable in Pakistani politics, " State of Martial Rule: Origins of Pakistan's Political Economy of Defence" ,1990)[23]. Many good books on global weapons sales in general and China in particular are accessible. Four books are worth mentioning. They are Anthony Sampson – "The Arms Bazaar"[24], 1977), "The Global Politics of Arms Sales" (1982)[25], Anne Gilks and Gerald Segal – "China and the Arms Trade" (1985[26]) and Michael Brozska and "Arms Transfers to the Third World: 1971" (1986)[27].

However, these book are really valuable books for studying the history of Chino Paks's ties and how it developed, and deals with the whole range of Chino Paks including military relations. Though there are numerous books on Pakistan's foreign policy, there are several here that merit special attention. 'Pakistan Foreign policy",[28] The book has a number of Indian publications and Pakistani writers such as S. P. Seth, Field Marshal Mohammed Auyub Khan, Khalid Bin Sayed ,Mohammed Haabib etc.. Two other notable books in this area are "Pakistan's Foreign Policy: An Historical Analysis", (1973[29]) and "Pakistan in Crisis", [30].

In addition, this work is based on contemporary discussion in the field of techno-politics and their securitisation relationship inside international relations to discuss how an infrastructure project like the CPEC form (in)safety. Therefore, it is essential to study the literature. The object of this analysis is double. First of all, the literary basis in techno-politics and its relation to the theory of securitization that is important for this study will be presented. Second, the academic divide with the theoretical context of technology and politics will be unveiled. Although several scholars presented in this review concentrated on the relationship between technology, regimes and (in) security, few examined the ties among techno-political infrastructure regimes and how they form insecurity. Infrastructure scientists have considered the infrastructure as referential artifacts, that is, the objects to be protected[31][32][33][34]. This research agrees with these scholars and considers infrastructural technological regimes a source of insecurity at the same time. In other terms, without removing the use of networks as a benchmark, we would broaden the manner in which infrastructure systems are seen as a possible security problem.

Through research into techno-politics, scientists have created hypotheses to help understand technology-policy interactions. The theory of techno-politics constitutes a significant basis as this study seeks to look at infrastructural technology and their effect on the safety discourse of the Indian Government. Techno-political scholars supported the idea by demonstrating the interaction of politics and technology. This segment presents the observations of these scientists and translates the techno-politics idea into foreign affairs and defence. Techno-power is described as 'hybrids of technological structures and political practises producing new modes of power and organisation[35]. Hecht also suggests that techno-politics is concerned with the usage of technologies to "constitute, reflect or promote political objectives[36].

It is important to remember that technology is not politics alone, but rather an "independent agent that is strategically suitable for various political purposes"[37]. Von Schnitzler[38] (2018) demonstrates how South African infrastructure was needed to maintain racial apartheid, and how it was created. Further, she claims that much of the protest tactics employed by the dominant community even after independence have been contained in the same infrastructure. Kurban et al. (2017)[39], in their analysis in techno-politics of ICT, find that the efforts of centralization and decentralisation, where various parties utilise ICT's in a different manner, are at stake. Both experiments suggest that various parties will exploit the autonomous technological organisation for different political purposes. Thus, with the technology as an item, the same technology has varying meanings with different players as well as a human contact with the artifact.

But technological politics does not have a single political ambition of its own region, which intersects with one technology. Rather than techno-politics, techno-political governments are involved. Technological and political regimes comprise of individuals interested with technologies, objects, political programmes, and philosophies who work together to further the regime's aim[40] . Crow-Miller et al. [41] revel in their essay "The techno-policy of big infrastructure and the Chinese water machine" these regimes and how they operate. They show the return of large water infrastructure in China, not as a revolutionary technology more developed than before but as an ideological regime, motivated by a longing for modernization and nation building, by past efforts to dominate nature (Ibid). Edwards and Hecht [42] also shows how South Africa helped legitimise the apartheid system by its Nuclear Techno-political regime through the Western power's fascination with nuclear power during the Cold War. These scholars demonstrate that technology regimes are not endogenous, but very well embedded in culture and influence and mirror the wider view of the social and political system[43].

The debate surrounding them is crucial to understand how the techno-political regimes construct, form, and constitute control. "Globalization Meets Frankenstein?" she asks in her post. In "Reflections on Terrorism, Nuclearity, and Global Technopolitical Discourse," Hecht provides an excellent argument for how post-9/11 discourses were influenced by Cold War techno-political hierarchies. She demonstrates the continuity of the "colonisers and colonised" discourse by applying a techno-political prism to the discourse around the nuclear non-proliferation system. The talk developed into a nuclear and a non-nuclear division and notes that the cross-linking ends in the Red States group and then into the 'axis of evil'

(Ibid). Here, Hecht shows the form, involve and difficulty of technology for political debate. These political discourses have been recognised as critical elements of foreign affairs[44]. Hence, techno-politics have now made their way into international relations.

In the debates within the area of international relations, the technology and techno-politics have for too long regarded technology as an isolated sector[45] . Technology experts have helped to grasp the competences that technology generates, shapes and maintains in the States, the regions, the countries and the transnationals. But it also forms the forces of technology through federal, geographic, domestic and transnational. Instantly, these scientists contend that technology, on the one side, influences world affairs in new ways, but also that global politics is shaping technology[46][47] . (Mayer et al.) Structured foreign affairs in techno-politics as: "How is science and technology affecting and changing the current organisations, structures, activities and actor? And how are they going to respond and adapt?' . These two issues form a strong basis for the analysis of the impact of the CPEC on the Indian government. But it is the point of this study that a dimension of securitisation must be introduced.

Though technology policy has moved rapidly to all domains of international affairs (see for example[48] Peters, Zittle, 2014), this work focuses on the insecurity of the Indian government in relation to the techno-political infrastructural regime of CPEC. As discussed earlier, scholars have considered infrastructure as referent artifacts rather than a securitized challenge to the quest for infrastructural technological regimes and (in) security. Other developments have nevertheless been thoroughly investigated in the region, the technical-political systems built around them and the impact on (in) security. This research presets more technology and its security implications, while the various innovations have different roles and are created for different purposes, as it clarifies the relationship between techno-policy regimes in general and (in) security.

In addition to research into the relationship between infrastructural technological systems and security, it should be noted that the two other techno-politic regimes (see for example[49][50]) are both nuclear. The author and his regimes contend that safety studies have ignored the position of technology in world politics. By moving technological theory into international relations, they work well to examine how (in) security in the region's, international and transnational arena is created, constituted and converted by technologies.

Nuclear safety authors contend that the global techno-political nuclear regime shapes the state's view of (in) security. Nuclear technology is particularly well positioned since it can both create one of the most stable energy sources whilst still leading to man's worst documented destruction[51]. In order to focus on science and technology, this places nuclear technology in a focus on (in)security. As Hecht[52] calls it, 'nuclear stuff' has a capacity for countries to interpret who creates (in)security by possession on a federal, foreign and transnational level. Hecht explains how technical risks intersubject, which means that technological safety threats are classified as discourse threats[53] (Buzan et al.)simply argues that, in the Gulf War or the Balkans, NATO or the United States do not use depleted uranium, it is not a nuclear danger, nor the states as North Korea or Iran as much as they dream of nuclear items one day. As Englert and Harrington[54] demonstrate, the link between nuclear techno-politics and (in)safety goes beyond warheads. The divide between military and civilian nuclear power is broken by Englert and Harrington as they argue that states or actors in the outside world no longer require a nuclear weapon. Rather it is enough to establish uncertainty through ownership of nuclear objects. What Englert and Harrington[55] shows is that an entity such as a "nuclear item" must not be scientifically harmful in order to establish a hazard of securitization but may be sufficiently menacing in its expression.

The cyberspace became increasingly disputed by various parties, and computer defence has attracted a lot of interest by many scientists. The authors dealing with cyber-security demonstrate how states are developing techno-political regimes capable of protecting themselves against potential assaults by examining cyber threats such as Stuxnet, attacks by the Iranian nuclear programme, and cyber-espionage by (other) nations. Hansen and Nissenbaum conclude in their document "Digital Disaster, Network Protection and the Copenhagen School" that cyber security must be seen in a wider range than security in the fields of military and physical security. They claim, in their post, that cyber attacks theoretically endanger other aspects of defence, such as daily security activities that contribute to hypersecurity . This reflects the manner in which the Copenhagen School sees protection as multi-dimensional, in the wider range of securitization.

The relationship between nuclear and cyber technologies, their systems and policies, as well as how they form (un)security, has been well studied. Nevertheless, scientists who are interested in the features and links to security of techno-political infrastructural regimes have yet to study these areas. The authors focused on the infrastructure rather than considering its infrastructure capabilities and organisations as potential risk producers, as referential artifacts, arguing that infrastructure is critical systems or key systems by means of techno-political regimes.

Infrastructure is an essential brand or crucial device by means of a voice securitisation act. Infrastructure thus is "seen to be endangered existentially and have a legal right to survive" (Buzan et al.). Scholars have focused on bio-political safety, and on the social and biological welfare of the people of a techno-political regime (Collier and Lakoff[56]). They claim that a state biopolitics is increasingly concerned about the value of maintaining access, flow and territorial power for the infrastructure . Any infrastructure that a technological-political regime considers necessary by speech securitization to ensure its population's welfare will therefore be the target of a techno political infrastructural system .

Overview: Literature gap

Techno-politics literature reviews and their security link have illuminated the construction and connections between technology-political regimes and security studies. The connection in techno-politics to security studies shows how various techno-political regimes shape (in) security, for example Carr, Hansen, Nissenbaum, Eriksson, Giacomello, Peoples, Englert, Harrington and Hecht. Nuclear and cyber safety research also helped to explain the relationship of technology to safety as a subjective and multi-dimensional one. But, as shown by the literature analysis, various systems provide various special capabilities. Therefore, information as to how such techno-political regimes (in)safety form to understand infrastructural regimes cannot be applied completely. Rather, the three specific infrastructure skills: connectivity, flow and territorial control are essential for their analysis.

Infrastructure scholars dealing with technological systems and safety based too much on seeing the infrastructure as reference. This is accomplished by concentrating on how the infrastructural techno-political systems ensure convergence, flow and territorial regulation. But study on how techno-political infrastructural regimes become a securitisation problem is not being done. Integrated with the theories of security and security studies established by scientists such as Collier, Lakoff, Cowen, Cavelty and Kristensen and how some techno-political regimes create insecurity . This study therefore sees infrastructural, technological and political regimes not only as referee subjects but also as securitized challenges by analyzing Sino-china relation and its effect on the security discourse of the Indian nation.

1.9 Chapterisation Scheme

Chapter 1

This chapter included a summary of the current study's relevant material, as well as a statement of the issue, research questions, the importance of the study, the objectives of the study, the scope of the study, and the research methodology. The first chapter often contains a survey of literature that was consulted by the scholar when preparing this study.

Chapter 2

This chapter would address the major theories of international affairs and seek to explain the partnership between China and Pakistan, as well as China and Pakistan's animosities against India. It will also attempt to discuss the transition and continuity in the India-China-Pakistan partnership.

Chapter 3

This chapter would go into the history of the Sino-Pak Axis and India since 1947.

Chapter 4

This chapter would go into the history of the triangle partnership, concentrating on the key conflicts, controversies, and collaboration. The second section of this chapter would concentrate on the main areas of cooperation between the two countries, namely China and Chapter 5

The chapter would, more specifically, concentrate solely on the consequences of the China-Pakistan alliance, emphasising security and geopolitical ramifications.

Chapter 6

This chapter will identify the key conclusions from the analysis report and will attempt to discuss the major initiatives and actions taken by all three countries to improve their partnership. After a short discussion of the findings, it will end with the potential possibilities of the three countries' alliance and their roles.

[1] Kenneth E. Boulding(1966), "Integrative Aspects of International System".

[2] Syed , A. (1969) "Sino-Pakistan Relations—An Overview"

[3] Kumar, S. (2007)"The China– Pakistan Strategic Relationship: Trade, Investment, Energy and Infrastructure"

[4] Haider, Z. (2005) "Sino-Pakistan relations and Xinjiang's Uighurs: Politics, trade, and Islam along the Karakoram highway"

[5] Lo, C. K. (2003)"China's Policy towards territorial disputes: the case of the South China Sea Islands"

[6] Deepak, B. R. (2006)" Sino-Pak 'Entente Cordiale and India A Look into the Past and Future"

[7] Deepak, B. R. (2006)"Sino-Pak 'Entente Cordiale and India A Look into the Past and Future"

[8] Kennedy, S. &. (2015) "Building China's 'One Belt, One Road'. Center for Strategic and International Studies"

[9] Singh, P. (2015) "The China Pakistan Economic Corridor and India"

[10] Pitlo III, L. B. (2015) "China's One Belt, One Road to Where?"

[11] Pehrson, C. J. (2006) "String of pearls: Meeting the challenge of China's rising power across the Asian littoral"

[12] Kukeyeva, F. T. (2012) "NEW FIVE DIMENSIONS OF GLOBAL SECURITY"

[13] Engardio, P. A. (2006) "The future of outsourcing"

[14] Khokhar, A. Y. (2011) "Sino-Indian relations: implications for Pakistan".

[15] Mirll, M. M. (2007) "Vigorous Cold War Handshakes: Reviewing Nixon's 1972 China Trip".

[16] Young, S. M. (2015) "US–China Relations"

[17] Malik, H. Y. (2012) "Strategic Importance of Gwadar Port"

[18] Kumar, S. (2007) "The China– Pakistan Strategic Relationship"

[19] Rajain, A. (2005) "Nuclear Deterrence in Southern Asia: China, India and Pakistan"

[20] Small, A. (2015) "The China-Pakistan Axis: Asia's New Geopolitics"

[21] Haider, Z. (2005) "Sino-Pakistan relations and Xinjiang's Uighurs: Politics, trade, and Islam along the Karakoram highway"

[22] Garver, J. W. (1996) " Sino-Indian Rapproachement and the Sino-Pakistan Entente".

[23] Ayesha Jalal - State of Martial Rule: Origins of Pakistan's Political Economy of Defence (1990)

[24] "The Arms Bazaar" (London: Hodder & Soughton, 1977)

[25] Andrew J. Pierre – "The Global Politics of Arms Sales" (New Jersey: Princeton Univ. Press, 1982).

[26] Anne Gilks and Gerald Segal – "China and the Arms Trade" (Sydney: Croom Helm, 1985)

[27] Michael Brozska and Thomas Ohlson – "Arms Transfers to the Third World: 1971" - 85 (SIPRI, London: OUP, 1986)

[28] "Pakistan Foreign policy", Hamid A. K. Rai (Aziz Publications : Lahore, 1981)

[29] S. M. Burke, "Pakistan's Foreign Policy: An Historical Analysis", (Oxford University Press, London, 1973)

[30] G. S. Bhargava, "Pakistan in Crisis", (Vikas, New Delhi, 1981)

[31] Collier, Stephen J. and Andrew Lakoff. 2008.
'The Vulnerability of Vital Systems: How "Critical Infrastructure"

[32] Savitzky, Satya and John Urry. 2015. "Oil on the Move".

[33] Cowen, Deborah. 2010a. "A Geography of Logistics: Market Authority and the Security of Supply Chains"

[34] Cavelty, Myriam Dunn. 2012. "The Militarisation of Cyber Security as a Source of Global Tension".

[35] Hecht, Gabrielle. 2010. "The Power of Nuclear Things".

[36] Hecht, Gabrielle. 2001. "Technology, Politics, and National Identity in France".

[37] Kurban, Can; Ismael Peña-López and Maria Haberer. 2017. "What is Technopolitics?

[38] Von Schnitzler, Antina. 2018. "Infrastructure, Apartheid Techno-politics, and Temporalities of 'Transition'"

[39] Kurban, et al., 2017. "What is Technopolitics? A Conceptual Schema for Understanding Politics in the Digital Age".

[40] Hecht, Gabrielle. 2001. "Technology, Politics, and National Identity in France".

[41] Crow-Miller, Britt; Michael Webber and Sarah Rogers. 2017. "The Techno-Politics of Big Infrastructure and the Chinese Water Machine"

[42] Edwards, Paul N. and Gabrielle Hecht. 2010. "History and the Technopolitics of Identity: The Case of Apartheid South Africa"

[43] Hecht, Gabrielle. 2001. "Technology, Politics, and National Identity in France".

[44] Chacko, Priya. 2019. "Constructivism and Indian Foreign Policy".

[45] Mayer, Maximilian; Mariana Carpes and Ruth Knoblich. 2014. "A Toolbox for Studying the Global Politics of Science and Technology"

[46] Mayer, Maximilian; Mariana Carpes and Ruth Knoblich. 2014. "A Toolbox for Studying the Global Politics of Science and Technology"

[47] Carr, Madeline. 2016. *US Power and the Internet in International Relations: The Irony of the Information Age*.

[48] Peters, Susanne and Werner Zittle. 2014. "The "Tight Oil Revolution" and the Misinterpretation of the Power of Technology"

[49] Carr, Madeline. 2016. *"US Power and the Internet in International Relations: The Irony of the Information Age"*.

[50] Hansen, Lene and Helen Nissenbaum. 2009. "Digital Disaster, Cyber Security, and the Copenhagen School".

[51] Englert, Matthias and Anne Harrington (2014) "How Much Is Enough? The Politics of Technology and Weaponless Nuclear Deterrence"

[52] Hecht, Gabrielle. 2010. "The Power of Nuclear Things".

[53] Buzan, Barry; Ole Wæver and Jaap de Wilde. 1998. *"Security: a New Framework for Analysis"*

[54] Englert, Matthias and Anne Harrington (2014) "How Much Is Enough? The Politics of Technology and Weaponless Nuclear Deterrence"

[55] Englert, Matthias and Anne Harrington (2014) "How Much Is Enough? The Politics of Technology and Weaponless Nuclear Deterrence"

[56] Collier, Stephen j. and Andrew Lakoff. 2015. "Vital Systems Security: Reflexive Biopolitics and the Government of Emergency".

CHAPTER II

Theoretical Framework

The theoretical structure on which this study is focused will be presented in this chapter. The thesis introduces its central theme, beginning with the theories of techno-political regimes, infrastructural techno-political systems and the challenge of securing infrastructure. The central idea is to mold (in)security by triggering a rhetoric of insecure from another political body whilst the infrastructural, technical-political system concentrates itself on telecommunications, and, by implication, access, flow and territorial power as the reference items. Finally, the chapter presents the philosophy of securitization of the Copenhagen School, which plays an essential role here.

Beijing has been involved in weapons transactions since the foundation of the People's Republic of China (PRC). Transfers were almost ignored during the early days, since they were very few, almost invariably free, and had little to no effect on the world weapons trade. The Chinese Communist Party, along with other countries, saw weapons transfer as a tool of its foreign policy after the communist victory in 1949. China also supplied arms for African and Latin American revolutionary revolutions and for communist rebels in neighbouring countries more closely. A few Communist nations, including Vietnam, North Korea and Albania, have had a special friendship with the PRC. Arms transfers to these countries took on additional importance as an instrument for external policy during the Sino-Soviet break in 1960.

In the 1960s, China's arms supplies are directly related to the foreign policy aims, plan and allies' choices. The main priorities were, for example, the need, after 1949, in the early phase of China, to protect against any global isolation and an impulse to promote nationalist revolutions and the "victory of the communist powers" in other nations. A critical change in Chinese strategy occurred in the early 1960s. The political background for this change is furnished by the Chinese-Soviet schism, and in general for Chinese stability and for its independent place in the world the need to reduce US power and get help in the SinoSoviet conflict was essential.

At the same moment, China has been supporting the unaligned nations in Asia for safety purposes, as well as the necessity of avoiding overt confrontations with the United States. In the 1960s, Islamabad and Beijing established a cordial agreement to address the common danger felt by both India and the Soviet Union. Following the 1965 Indo-Pak War and the US weapons embargo on Pakistan, Islamabad became a significant receiver of Chinese arms. Though the free military aid was severely undermined, China maintained its strategy until Mao died in 1976. Subsequently, the Chinese defence industry started to market with Deng Xiaoping's rise to power in 1978 and the subsequent reforms and China joined the international market for weapons as an arms dealer. However, China has certain distinctive characteristics, unlike other weapons trading nations. The first feature is that the indigenous manufacturing of Chinese weapons influences the arms trade policies of other states in East and South Asia because of its position in heart of Asia. China must also be understood in the widest context as a weapons supplier - both as an exporter and as an incentive to imports from its neighbours. Second, China is distinguishing because, in contrast to the other large weapons exporting countries, it is a developing world with a much less advanced arms industry.

Chinese exporters have also sought to persuade recipients that inexpensive and less advanced infrastructure is the only way forward. China's third distinctive feature is that even if it is one of the leading weapons-exporting nations, it is not capable of selling arms to other developing countries. Beijing relies almost entirely on markets for its weapons shipments in the developed world. Chinese transfers of weapons are notably characterised by China becoming highly dependent on the economies of the Middle East, as were most other arms exporting countries. It is also not, save for Pakistan, the primary producer of weapons for its main markets. Though Pakistan is the largest recipient of Chinese weapons, China has succeeded in preventing excessive export dependency on any state. China initially sold weapons mainly on ideological and 'friendship prices' considerations. In his initial location, though, there subsequently was a dramatic change and weapons were sold for benefit.

China demonstrated its willingness to sell traditional weapons in its arsenal and showed little hesitation in supplying weapons to all sides in a dispute (In the Iran-Iraq War). Of course, in general, Chinese firearms are less modern and efficient than those marketed by developing countries. Clearly, Chinese machinery is not a first class, but it is more than a third rate. The very conditions leading to demand and Pakistan's formation contained the source of the new State's increasing military strength.

Pakistan as a nation-state was founded on the premise and philosophy of war with parent state, culture and subcontinent civilization. Pakistan was unfortunately unable to develop sound democratic structures, mainly because of the same number of reasons. That in return contributed swiftly to the military interference in the state's political power base, which has persisted over the last five decades with adjustments here and there. Over the past years, a link has developed with the establishment of a military-bureaucratic feudal elite, capturing and controlling the political base of Pakistan. This leading élite has a strong interest in taking an opposing position against India in order to maintain its prestige and hang on to the power base of the country. In this way, it became absolutely important to generate and perpetuate Pakistan's image of a 'political danger from India.' A convergence of these two has contributed to the production on one hand and the militarization of its foreign policy, on the other, of a strong military machine. Increasing and maintaining military strength has become one of Pakistan's key pillars, especially injuring the search for military and strategic external aid. Pakistan has challenged its partners and entered into partnerships in this context. Pakistan wanted to align themselves with the USA in light of the prevalent global situation immediately following its division. But Pakistan soon was disillusioned with its Super Power partner because of the United States' unwillingness and unwillingness in any instance to support the Pakistani "viewpoint." The past of the military ties between the Sino-Park began there, which could be assumed to date back to 1963 in which they signed a boundary agreement. However, Pakistan turned favourably to China when the US imposed a weapons embargo on China in late September 1965.

2.1 Regimes Of Techno-Political

The CPEC is a long way from the only techno-political infrastructural infrastructure in Pakistan and South Asia. The theoretical framework of technopolitical regimes is used in this study to capture and analyse the technopolitical CPEC mechanism except for other infrastructures developed in Pakistan and South Asia. It is often argued in principle that CPEC is the technology and device of the techno-policy infrastructure, providing CPEC with a capability to control the Indian government's security speech in the way it does.

The technological regimes are institutionalised systems consisting of individuals associated with the technology, the objects, political processes and philosophies that work together to achieve a political objective, as previously mentioned[1]. Gabrielle Hecht coined the term "techno-political systems" in her essay "Technology, Politics, and National Identity in France" It helps to understand how politics can pursue a political purpose through technology, while also helping to understand how technology influences politics. Thus, techno-political governments are understood as "hybrid techniques and political practises that generate modern modes of force and agency."[2] (Edwards and Hecht 2010, 619). The way citizens link technology and politics both discursively and materially in a technopolitical regime has its consequences[3]. As such, investigation into what a technopolitical regime says is not sufficient, and thus it is important to examine what kind of technology is made, why it is created, how it is produced and where it is produced.

Hecht claims that the metaphor of the dictatorship shows three different aspects between technological hybridity and politics . First, she asserts that she emphasises not only the technological objects but the people and ideologies which shape the artefacts, through naming them government. Second, Hecht and other scholars involved in techno-political regimes have shown that the regimes do not impose on some tradition or political system. In other words, government decisions and speeches are guided by a wider socio-political order. Thirdly, Hecht (2001) states that techno-political regimes must cope with critiques if they emerge inside or from outside government according to scholars such as Kuban et al.[4] and von Schnitzler [5], who argue that same technology has a different setting and rhetoric for different players (258). Thus, techno-political regimes are not undisputed (Ibid).

Using the analysis definition of the technology regimes, CPEC may be seen, rather than rhetorically or technologically, as a mixture of politics and technology. The three distinct features of Hecht's technopolitical regimes must be understood. This means that researchers should study, and how it is treated in an exogenous way, not just CPEC as a techno-policy regime. As defined by the theoretical model of techno-politics and three distinct features of Hecht, CPEC consists of infrastructural technology. Thus, the following aspect of the technological-political framework will examine the specific capacity of techno-political regimes in infrastructure.

2.2 Infrastructural Techno-Political Regimes

The techno-political regime of CPEC is focused on technology of infrastructure. Therefore it is essential to examine the distinct characteristics of infrastructure technologies. As already mentioned, infrastructure technology is characterised as transport, supply of essential goods, and public or private facilities required for everyday living[6]. As a socio-technical construction, infrastructure does not provide one direction, but provides a forum for the technological-political system to change the environment (Folkers 2017, 858). Although infrastructure is its own technology, it is the regime's responsibility to determine whether and how infrastructure is constructed. While technology for a paved road would provide the capacity for heavy transport, the road is paved from, where paved, where paved, how large should the paved road and so on is up to the infrastructural techno-political regime.

- Infrastructure researchers also shown that they have three distinct yet intertwined characteristics: coordination, flow and territorial power: The premise of technology as socio-technical promotes a knowledge that, while infrastructure serves as a means of contact, transmission and territorial control, it is up to the techno-political system to decide where and when it is necessary to allow connection, flow and territorial control. In terms of Coordination, Flow and Territorial Control, understanding of techno-political infrastructural systems needs three concepts:
- Connectivity is the enabling of *"[the] interaction between socially diverse and often spatially dispersed 'communities of practice' [...] and allow for the emergence of national or even transnational political collectives"*. In order for technical political regimes to expand in this region, infrastructure acts not only within the State but also across frontiers, which enables transnational cooperation and transnational flows. Infrastructure, thus, has the potential to get two or more political institutions closer together through its techno political regimes.
- Flow can be interpreted as the opportunity to continually get "thing". Thus, things, from resources to other commodities and persons or thoughts, could be everything. Ensure that things arrive on time and continue is important for a state's functions[7].
- Territorial power, by communication and flow, is the capacity to create an infrastructural technopolitical regime: *"penetrate civil society, and to implement logistically political decisions throughout the realm"*[8]. The technological-political structure place and seize control in a nation[9] .Mann claim that constructing infrastructure is a way for states, by daily life infrastructure and therefore country-based residents, to gain land and citizens possession. In areas which are controversial by two nations

such as the Kashmir region, the infrastructure not only acts as a population regulation, it also acts as a counter-government power.

2.3 Repercussions for India

There is a lot of basic competition and bilateral mistrust and suspicion in the history of Sino-India and Indo-Pakistan. In the light of insecurity, Chinese-Indian ties are limited by the ensuing challenges facing both States that reveal tensions.

The territorial dispute

China is a vast country. Through eighteen nations, China has territorial and frontier tensions. The exception is Pakistan's Islamic Republic, which it maintains on its payroll.

Sino-Pak relations

China-Pakistan ties are another repercussion for India. China and Pakistan are "all-weather neighbours," with shared support and collaboration. They have kept in touch and are acquainted with each other. Over time and distance, these relationships have been put to the test. Despite the significant changes that have occurred on the world and regional stages, their joint corporation has grown in power and vitality, and it has also been untouched by domestic changes. The ties between the two countries are based on respect for the ideals of the charter of the United Nations and the five principles of peaceful cohabitation[10] . It is focused on mutual conviction and confidence and was nurtured and reinforced by daily experiences of high standard. Both parties have a common interest in and have cooperated to accomplish this aim in South Asia for peace and stability. They reject transnational and racial hegemony and have fought toward a just global imperative, both political and commercial. Pakistan and China consult on their issues on a regular basis and participate in international and regional fora. It is often hoped that the relations between the two countries would flourish and strengthen, in particular in the upcoming period.

CPEC and India's stance

China-Pakistan agreed to build a China Pakistan corridor during the Musharraf era, known as the economic corridor China Pakistan (CPEC). In Xinjiang Uygur, China, it links Kashgar with the port of Gwadar in southwest Pakistan (Baluchistan) . India protested the corridor as it passes through Pakistan's contested Azad Kashmir region. Furthermore, it is possible that some in China, India and Pakistan also have to settle very severe territorial conflicts. If the CPEC is inventive, though, new panoramas

of local economic cooperation and peace would be opened up in the area[11]
.

In response to the Gwadar Kashgar scheme, a changing regional climate provides the Indian policymakers with many options: First, India can continue to object and demonstrate, but it cannot resist, that could delay or impede building the corridor (CPEC). Second, by extending to Pakistan and China to suggest trilateral cooperation in the proposed construction, India may follow a more positive approach on corridor. Between India and Pakistan there are already some ties. Such trilateral cooperation (China-India-Pakistan) could eventually trigger regional economic co-operation, regional integration and the growth of human resources. The only "game changeers" in the world are the economic highways between China and South Asia.

Regional ambitions

By implementing policies on influence in India, China will expand its influence in India (Levine)[12] and (Pehrson)[13]. China's policy of circumcision with India, is reacted by New Delhi's "look at East scheme"[14] , development of its ties with Taiwan, Japan, Vietnam, etc. Both States are entitled to be recognised as regional and local influence as a result of their tremendous economic growth. Both countries are fighting to match the military game, but they are playing a multi-sum game[15] . For India, the chance to move into Afghanistan, to better the huge Central Asian flea market and to have access to the excessive natural resources of the area will be greatly enhanced by such cooperation, which has been a dream of India. Pakistan will also have huge advantages in this regard. The antagonism towards India will also cease[16].

Global ambitions:

There are also global targets for China and India. China has been less arguing and leads close diplomacy and India has strong plans to play a global position. In the United Nations Security Council, India and Japan requested a veto power position. However, India assured its crucial presence in the UNSC to be enhanced by establishing a five plus community consisting of five permanent representatives plus two temporary members. India's global aspirations are constantly verified by China[17].

2.4 Securitization Theory

Securitization theory, also regarded as the "Copenhagen school," has evolved into a powerful and complex tool for examining security discourses and their connection to security practise. In the research on border defence, this thesis aims to exploit advances in theory of securitization in both Pakistan and China (PRC). The area of securitisation is suitable for these subject-matters because of their potential to participate both explicitly and within the framework of wider current discussions in IR[18] . This pushes security research outside the conventional readings of traditionally strategic affairs that rely on the military and the state. This will allow the 'expansion of the study agenda through new economic, environmental, cultural and security sectors - communities, NGOs, individuals'[19]. This renders CS suitable in every location for considering dynamic safety connections. In principle, both themes I would raise are: First, how can a theory of securitization apply to non-liberal or non-democratic systems and how can it be implemented without over expanding its key principles. Secondly, how do we use extended philosophy of securitisation outside the traditional methods of language? First of all, I will outline the CS-Security Paradigm with its key principles and methodologies and illustrate challenges.

2.4.1 The Copenhagen School

The Copenhagen School (CSmain)'s advocates, Ole Wver and Barry Buzan, describe securitization as:

"[A successful speech act] through which an inter-subjective understanding is constructed within a political community to treat something as an existential threat to a valued referent object, and to enable a call for urgent and exceptional measures to deal with the threat" .

The securitization theory thesis aims to raise debate as a significant part of the examination of defence. The CS is based on the theory of speech acts and illocutionary strands of reasoning to analyse this discourse. Defense is therefore based on the fundamental supposition that a new institutional structure is created by a declaration of the security system itself, which is bracketing "natural politics." This is founded on speech actions in which an agent securitising designates and announces an existential hazard to a given reference objective, which implies that exceptional means must be used to prevent it. The problem of the securitization precedes a security problem which, if an audience believes the argument, shows the "security," thereby allowing a person a freedom to break rules which would otherwise be obligatory[20] .According to the argument, three constitutive factors or "felicity requirements" are needed for securitization to succeed: 1) the grammar or plot of protection 2) the enunciator's social wealth, and 3) hazard factors . Within that specific context, every securitizing agent must immediately obey certain laws, that is, the language creation, by those individuals and situations, of an existential hazard in relation to a referent entity. If these laws are not followed, securitisation is incomplete.

Two core problems need to be highlighted and improved in the CS. First of all, the question of "natural politics" vs. This divisions are the historical "democratic distinctions" of the SC and therefore a possible restricting factor. Secondly, the CS' "felicity requirements" provide an excessive degree of formality, namely, that the system proposes a discursive safety act. This dependence on the given criteria of the "speech act" "lends itself too much to a twisted sense of [securitization] as having a set, permanent, unchanging [code of practise]," according to the critic[21]. This over-reliance on speech acts restricts protection to traditional protocol, in which felicity requirements must be met in their entirety for the securitization act to succeed1.

2.4.2 Speech Act Theory

The CS school of study is founded on speech act theory, as established by John L. Austin (1975) and John Searle (1969). When premised on the idea that a speech act may constitute a security problem, securitizing language is called generalizable. These processes may be simplified to a series of practical ruses, which should be applicable to all cultures. Language is governed by laws, and if limited to practical rules, they should be uniformly applicable regardless of situation. As a result, language usage is regulated by laws, and all human languages share a collection of constitutive rules that reside underneath traditional semantic frameworks. Language as a skill logically precedes a particular conventional manifestation of it. Human languages are therefore known as "different traditional realisations of the same fundamental rules" when they are inter-translatable[22]. When political rhetoric is classified as speech acts, it is believed that such statements go beyond simply representing a given fact and, as a result, cannot be measured as valid or false. These remarks can be seen as "performative" rather than "constrictive."

In speech act review, there are three sections to remember. "1) The locutionary: the utterance of a word containing a specific meaning and reference". 2) The illocutionary act: the act of articulating a locution (Ibid). This group "captures the overt performative class of utterances, and in particular, the term 'speech act' is practically predicated on that sort of agency". Finally, 3) the perlocutionary: these are the "consequential consequences that are aimed at evoking emotions, opinions, ideas, or behaviours in the target audience" .Habermas summarises this trifecta of categories as "to say something, to participate in saying something, to bring about something by acting in saying something."

The second one is 'unique to the circumstances under which the proceedings are made and hence not traditionally reached through uttering a certain utterance and comprises all those results which, whether intended or unintentional, are sometimes indeterminate, that certain particular utterances may trigger in a particular situation. The illusionary (i.e. an act of saying something), Thierry Balzacq says here, is conflicted with perlocutionary (i.e. an act of saying something) . This strategy decreases the security of the speaker's actions without making space for the public. Balzacq aims to increase the audience's role in securitisation by questioning over dependence on the role of the speaker. By recognising this aim, securitisation may be best applied in a range of non-western ways to new markets.

2.4.3 Theoretical Problems

Many of the major theoretical questions relating to CS schools can be addressed while dealing with China and Pakistan's case studies. The main issues identified in this research are the responsibility for political prejudice, distinguishing common from special politics and applying strategic pragmatics in order to better establish a securitisation theory.

Democratic Bias

The general applicability of securitisation to non-liberal or non-democratic governments, a concern emanating from the past[23], and the trend towards 'historical and euro-centric arrogance' as Buzan and Little once named it. The point is that this leads to a political prejudice in the philosophy of securitisation.

Security problems are necessarily interpreted as a type of particular politics in this sense, which legitimises particular procedures as a means of survival. Vuvori argues that this formulation implies an ethical movement for democracy, de-security is imperative (Ibid). Therefore in order to become a wide-ranging and applicable paradigm for security analysis, securitization studies must actively address security speech and policy in every kind of policy structure. One difficulty in particular is the need to attain a massive degree in cultural literacy to analyse securitization studies beyond a democratic liberal situation. Adopting this mentality leads IR towards emerging areas of expertise, which is today certainly likely because colleges are increasingly interconnected. This makes IR less dependent on reductions in realism and game theory; nevertheless, it makes it increasingly challenging to establish a normative structure.

Normal vs. Special Politics

A central difference in the CS lies between regular politics and special politics (security/emergency). The 'defence,' according to the CS, is the movement which takes politics outside the rules of the game and frames the question either as a particular policy or as a political one. Securitization should also be used as a more radical political variant[24]. Those definitions need to be discussed more. "Special policies" were described to include (1) non-political topics beyond the competence of the State; (2) political questions that are on the agenda for "daily politics". The second of the three mostly applies to non-democratic decisions that are taken in the context of survival need. The dilemma is that this formulation considers unique politics to be something that is outside the process of democracy. In a non-liberal democratic regime, protection considerations do not need to be brought into the specific conception of special politics, since no democratic mechanism begins. But that's not really the case. The requirement here is that authority be preserved since this is essential if any social organisation is to survive and any government must commit actions of persuasion and manipulation to survive. This applies in Pakistan and in the PRC, with both democratic and non-democratic regimes. Also the most authoritarian governments must legitimise the usage of extraordinary action for all cultures. It needs to be interpreted contextually as this definition of "unique politics." We may argue that all communities have regulations which are the "products of historical and social contingency, as are items and protection risks". If protection reasoning is used to crack these laws, we may maintain that securitization is an observed case .While democratic mechanisms are the limits to be violated in a democratic system, it is merely a question of defining the related restrictions in a non-democratic society. However, the main problem is the differentiation between "common" and "private" politics. The army and intelligence (ISI) possess a great deal of power and authority in Pakistan, for example, but they remain very confidential. The political structures of the Chinese Communist Party (CCP) remain hidden and therefore a similar issue continues while researching Chinese politics.

Strategic Pragmatics

As pointed out, a key principle I want to deal with is that the CS is highly formal, and it fails to take adequate account of the public in security issues. The above factor of the CS should not be underlined in an effort to relegate the principle of speech acts, but rather as 'strategic intervention'[25]. This varies since the perspective of the rhetoric of defence leads to a degree of belief that uses objects such as metaphor, feelings, stereotypes, gestures or even silence, which makes for more relative interpretation or contextual analysis . A philosophical question arises from this extension of theory: how can a consistent, broadly accessible structure are maintained to take account of special features and acts which are quite cultural and contextual? We will see CS School as a universal pragmatic to further conceptualise this for the overall purpose of establishing a regulatory system for study of safety discourses. This normative goal is potentially limiting in considering regimes beyond a Western model which means the big variation in the major socio-political standards, including those sure to arise in cases of Pakistan and the PRC, outside liberal democracy – and the associated political and social conditions – is likely to lead to a rare fulfilment of the conditions of congratulations This should not be seen, though, as a result of securitization. The psychological strategy can use qualitative hints to detect how a target audience's persuasion works. If this conviction is seen as a mandate to defeat or to mitigate the danger found, securitisation can be carried out. The extent of the performance of a speech act can not be determined by obedience to the traditional laws that actors obey, but rather by "... a discursive approach enabling [public] mind adherence to the thesis submitted to its agreement to be induced or increased by the actor securitizing" .Through recognising the possible limitations of normative constraints, particularly in the cases examined in the study, an expanded concept of a securitization study can be looked at where the security discourse is approached to a social context in which the securitisation players concentrate on a safety issue and move the audience to support policy alignment .

[1] Hecht, Gabrielle. 2001. "Technology, Politics, and National Identity in France".

[2] Edwards, Paul N. and Gabrielle Hecht. 2010. "History and the Technopolitics of Identity: The Case of Apartheid South Africa"

[3] Hecht, Gabrielle. 2001. "Technology, Politics, and National Identity in France".

[4] Kurban, et al., 2017. "What is Technopolitics? A Conceptual Schema for Understanding Politics in the Digital Age".

[5] Von Schnitzler, Antina. 2018. "Infrastructure, Apartheid Technopolitics, and Temporalities of 'Transition'"

[6] Edwards, Paul N. and Gabrielle Hecht. 2010. "History and the Technopolitics of Identity: The Case of Apartheid South Africa"

[7] Cowen, Deborah. 2010a. "A Geography of Logistics: Market Authority and the Security of Supply Chains"

[8] Mann, Michael. 1984. "The Autonomous Power of the State, its Origins, Mechanisms and Results".

[9] Mukerji, Chandra. 2010. "The Territorial State as a Figured World of Power : Strategics , Logistics , and Impersonal Rule"

[10] Deepak, B. R. (2006)" Sino-Pak 'Entente Cordiale and India A Look into the Past and Future"

[11] Small, Andrew. 2015. *"The China-Pakistan Axis: Asia's New Geopolitics"*.

[12] Levine, J. H. (1972). "The sphere of influence"

[13] Pehrson, C. J. (2006). *"String of pearls: Meeting the challenge of China's rising power across the Asian littoral"l*.

[14] Jaffrelot, C. (2003). "India's look east policy: an Asianist strategy in perspective".

[15] Kukeyeva, F. T. (2012). "NEW FIVE DIMENSIONS OF GLOBAL SECURITY"

[16] Egreteau, R. (2008). "India's Ambitions in Burma: More Frustration Than Success??".

[17] Winters, A. &. (2007). *"Dancing with giants: China, India, and the global economy"*. .

[18] Williams, Michael C. (2003) "Words, Images, Enemies: Securitization and International Politics"

[19] Guzzini Stefano and Dietrich Jung (eds.) (2004) "Contemporary Security Analysis and Copenhagen Peace Research".

[20] Wæver, Ole (1995) "Securitization and Desecuritization".

[21] Balzacq, T. (2005)"The Three Faces of Securitization: Political Agency, Audience and Context"

[22] Searle, John, and Daniel Vanderveken. 1985. *"Foundations of illocutionary logic"*

[23] Vuori, J. A. (2008). "Illocutionary Logic and Strands of Securitization: Applying the Theory of Securitization to the Study of Non-Democratic Political Orders".

[24] Buzan, Barry (1983) "People, states, and fear: the national security problem in international relations"

[25] Balzacq, T. (2005) "The Three Faces of Securitization: Political Agency, Audience and Context"

31

[25] Balzacq, T. (2005) "The Three Faces of Securitization: Political Agency, Audience and Context"

CHAPTER III

Historical Background of Sino–Pak Axis and India

3.1 Introduction

This chapter will provide a historical background on Pakistan-China ties. Both the countries belonged to ancient cultures and their contact had provided both the countries a sense of centuries old shared heritage. This chapter will trace the events previous to the inception of Pakistan on August 14, 1947 and declaration of Peoples Republic by China on October 1, 1949. The major event in Pakistan's case is the 23 March 1940 day on which Pakistan resolution calling for a separate nation to be adopted for the Muslims in the Subcontinent and the establishment of the Communist Party of China (CPC) for China on July 21, 1921. CPC was a political group that came to power in 1949 and had managed to rule China up to the present days. The historical viewpoint has therefore centred on the evolution of interactions from non-entities and freshly born entities.

In order to know China's potential actions and its world view, it will be necessary to take a deeper look at its past. Michael D Swaine maintained that national pride, appearance of peace loving polity alongside virtuous central government and mutually beneficial vision of interstate ties have affected China's thinking and actions[1] , which in turn impacted on China's incremental perception of the world and manifesting in its foreign policy behaviour as well. China's situation will be a complicated illustration since its behaviour has varied across different epochs of history. Certain Chinese would see the Western world as hegemon of vested interests but also others would respect their ideals and traditions. [2]It is primarily due to this very complexity of China's actions that drawing some generalisation regarding China's political behaviour and its worldview will be challenging.

Here, it can be added that the experience of a nation will be vital to understand the effect of time and culture on person or social behaviour and the expectations of the general population of that country. Other factors in human nature being equivalent, societies particularly ideology, traditions, arts, language, theory, historical modes of war and peace will turn a given community inhabiting a certain landscape. It will, however, be vital to analyse the effect of history as well as cultural changes on the population to explain the behaviour trends of the state as a whole. This perspective will be important to China as well.

With a population of 1.39 billion people, China will be the most populous nation in the world, accounting for 19.24% of the world population. The Chinese GDP growth in 2014 reached 7.4 percent in 2014, as opposed to the expectation of 7.5 percent, according to an economic survey. August[3] China has seen unparalleled growth indicators over the last few decades which have managed to get over 500 million people out of poverty.

China's existence dates back to prehistory. It was subsequently dominated by ancient dynasties and empires that governed China's political structure. Historically, Chinese culture has been split into ancient, colonial and contemporary China in ancient times. The Paleolithic period that was the Old Stone Age and the Nelithic era that was the Modern Stone Age is prehistoric. Late Palaeolithic days were about ten thousand to forty thousand years,[4] and Neolithic periods were about the Yangtze River and Yellow River at the age of around seventy thousand years.

Kashmir became the flashpoint after Pakistan was established, while other disputes arose as far as partitioning concerned. A friction between the princely ruler and his Muslim people became fighting. The insurgency started in Poonch after turmoil in Jammu. On 22nd October 1947, illegal Pakistani soldiers crossed the princely state along with tribal militias. Jammu and Kashmir's Hindu leader signed an instrument of accession with India that Pakistan considered unfair. Just weeks after they started, both newborn states went to fight. There was a truce, but the matter remained an inconsistent problem that could have disastrous consequences in the region. In view of the fighting, Pakistan and India have tended to strain ties and have engaged in conflicts, including in Kashmir in 1948, in War in 1965, in War in 1971, and in Kargil in 1999.

Pakistan and China were once again confronted with issues. Both countries have a lot with initial years of difficulty. [5]Pakistan was confronted with various problems such as financial allocations, border demarcations, demographic transfer, in addition to a massive genocide of Muslim refugees, princely annexed states and invasion. Pakistan faced several problems. China confronted the challenges posed in the world by years of civil war. In addition to unemployment, hunger, food shortages and demographic development the Chinese government had to contend with

increasing inflation, corruption, analphabetism and inequalities. [6]These
problems presented Chinese leadership with enormous challenges. In brief,
during their developing political identity and nationality unification, China
and Pakistan faced a series of challenges and problems. They seemed to be
able to appreciate each other and that their interactions had an effect on
their bilateral relationship at this stage.

The People's Republic of China was declared by China in 1949. It has
become a big period of world history. The second world war has just
finished and the world was adapting to the improvements that had taken
place in the political and economic field owing to a long war. The war
broke the economies and the diplomatic impact, in particular, of major
European powers. Again, a number of new States became autonomous and
new partnerships were established to resolve the problems of the
sovereignty. Soon there came into being two fragmentary centres of
influence and the universe was split into two blocks. The US and the Soviet
Union led one bloc. The effects of these global developments were also
experienced by Pakistan and China, making strategic decisions, and
correcting some of the policies they have quickly adopted. Therefore, it is
not surprising that the ties between Pakistan and China have seen up- and
downs until they have been solid and useful to each other.

Phases of History of Pakistan-China Relations (1949-1990).

The three phases of ties between Pakistan and China from 1949 until
1990 can be understood as, the first stage of the reluctance and aversion
would be identified as (1949-1961). During this era, both countries
measured their hesitation, mainly because of their ideological foundations
and the political global climate. Phase two, characterised by reconciliation
and empathy, started with the boundary war between India and China.
Pakistan took Pakistan and China closer together, as did the war in India and
China and the US-China rapprochement mediated by Pakistan. Friendship
and cordiality is the third period of Pakistan-China ties (1979-1990).
During this time, major political changes have taken place, such as the
Soviet invasion of Afghanistan and the declining Soviet presence in Eastern
Europe. In this period of Pakistan-China ties, economic and political
cooperation between Pakistan and China was also strengthened. The
following three phases are explored.

3.2 Phase of Reluctance and Aversion (1949-1961)

With regard to bilateral ties between Pakistan and China, a time of
reluctance and aversion could be identified from 1949 to 1961. The greatest

factors in Pakistan-China relations are ideological foundations, stronger relationships between India and USSR and India and China, the expansion of Pakistan-US links, Pakistan's security concerns and an unpredictable global politics landscape. Pakistan and China ideologically took a separate approach because of the political conflict at the beginning of Pakistan when the CPC rose to power by means of a Communist base movement. After independence, the country faced an incertain and unpredictable global political environment as a result of its united Pakistan's alliances which took Pakistan to the US or the western camp. In this time the ties between Pakistan and China remained reticent and aversive.

Initially, ties between Pakistan and China appeared odd, since both countries had distinct philosophies and had stood by. The struggle leading to Pakistan's creation was focused on Islamic philosophy, in which the Muslims of the subcontinent were seeking a separate nation, with religious, social and economic freedom. In contrast, modern China was led by the CPC and its fight was based on Communist principles, emphasising people's essential needs and defending their liberty. [7]When China took a democratic direction and Pakistan pursued a constitutional path, the distinction between the two countries became obvious. Liberal philosophy was also in conflict with Pakistan's potential ideals. It is true that there existed since ancient times a territorial relationship between Pakistan and China, but in tradition, society, political structure or faith the two states were less than united. [8]In view of these disparities, Pakistan remembered and acknowledged the importance of China.

Pakistan was among the first countries to recognise the PRC when Pakistan's ambassador to the Soviet Union for China, Mr Chou En Lai, sent a note on 5 January 1950 announcing that Pakistan recognised its PRG as the legitimate government. As follows, on 29 January 1950, the decision to revoke recognition from the Kumintang (KMT) Government in Taiwan by Pakistan was communicated to the China Ambassador in the Soviet Union[9]. [10]By formally acknowledging China, Pakistan then ceased to have ties with Taiwan. It also backed China's case for United Nations Security Council participation (UNSC). In that context, the United Nations General Assembly (UNGA's) issued a statement on 25 September 1950 by Mohammad Zafar Ullah Khan. Pakistan became the first Muslim nation to develop diplomatic ties with China, the second Commonwealth country and its three non-communist countries, on May 21, 1951.

Pakistan and China started their journeys in a foreign setting separated into two opposing blocs: the Eastern bloc led by the Soviet Union and the Western bloc led by the United States. The conflict within these blocs was attributed to their different communist and capitalist philosophies. [11]Pakistan and China are geographically similar, since they are in the immediate vicinity of their opponents and therefore form their regional and global issues. Whereas Pakistan had unfriendly ties with both Afghanistan and India at the time, the country shared frontier with Japan, India and the Soviet Union. At its inception, the ties with its neighbours have always been a worry for their welfare. Both countries were confronted with territorial sovereignty questions.

India had friendly relations with China in the beginning of the 1950's, while Pakistan remained distant from China. Although their ties have been greatly influenced by two subsequent events. The Non-Aligned Movement (NAM) was one of the main elements that formed the positive relations between China and India and the West as a result of Pakistan's choice to enter into security alliances. In 1954 Pakistan was incorporated into the organisation of the South East Asia Treaty (SEATO); in 1955 Pakistan was joined by the Central Treaty Organization (CENTO) to check the communist growth, not doing good with the Chinese and creating a distance between the two countries. The slogan, "Indians and Chinese Brothers, are brothers." Nevertheless, China has retained friendly ties with Pakistan because of its willingness to encourage good relations with its neighbouring countries and Chinese perception of Pakistan-India aggression, and of Pakistan's restrictions.

On 19 May 1954, a Mutual Defense Assistance Agreement between the US and Pakistan was signed240. Pakistan was signed on 8 September 1954 with US-backed SEATO support. Pakistan entered the Baghdad Pact on 23 September 1955. Later it was called CENTO, 241 SEATO, though CENTO, in the Middle East and West East, aims to defeat communism. Pakistan's aim to enter those alliances was to protect its own position vis-à-vis India, motivated by security calculations. The US was tilted against India in Pakistan as US economic assistance to India rose in 1957.242 These alliances, as the later one signed them, were diplomatic counterproductive for Pakistan at the expense of receiving anger from significant neighbours. Pakistan remained mostly unfulfilled and disappointed with the hopes expressed by these alliances[12].

Pakistan faced the risk of irritating and disliking the Soviet Union in China. Both were major neighbours of Pakistan. The US and the West regarded the alliances as an instrument in disabilities for communism in South East Asia, South West Asia and the Middle East, and for it to expand its influence.[13] Pakistan signed these alliances expecting US assistance in Jammu and Kashmir issues, to earn economic income and solve the problem of the waters of Indus. Pakistan wanted to win the US against Indian hegemony as an ally, above all.[14] Pakistan had not benefited much from its alliances. Rather, these led to a confrontation risk for Pakistan with the Soviet Union, in particular, because of the issue of the U 2 spy plane. The US has also failed to honour its obligations to comply in the event of war with India, and no agreement has been invoked.246 These treaties and agreements were to be brought to their natural disappearances, when it has become evident that the superpower, and not the smaller Member States, unilaterally benefits their provisions. This was largely because the US was concerned with global security concerns, while the security interests of Pakistan were regional.

Pakistan and China have been forced into competing blocs, driven by certain geo-policy limitations. Pakistan entered the partnerships supported by the USA and the Western countries and went to the West's fold. By contrast, China backed the Soviet Union, leading the communist bloc. Once again, Pakistan had to seek confidence to preserve itself in the face of its territorial integrity challenges, while China became an alliance with the Soviet Union on the basis of common ideology and similar global and regional political perceptions. While these defence alliances paid Pakistan huge military support between 1953 and 1961, it cost the imposition of trade sanctions and the resulting distance to Pakistan of China and the Soviet Union. Pakistan and China were able to continue to establish regular ties despite these difficulties and inconsistencies. During this time, the tendency of Pakistan toward the US and China towards India did not warm enough ties between Pakistana and China.

Security partnerships have therefore thrown a shadow in the development of Pakistan-China ties. The US repeatedly reiterated that the expansion of communism requires these alliances. In the search for world dominance, the United States saw the Soviet Union as a significant competition. The US often saw China as an ideologically based partner of the Soviet Union. The extension of the influence of the Soviet Union and China was challenged when faced with communism. For its own safety and survival needs, Pakistan had entered these defence alliances. During the Conference on Bandung, which was recognised in its declaration on 23 April 1955, the Chinese Prime Minister Zhou Enlai explained his stance. He spoke of the Pakistani Prime Minister's statement that Pakistan had signed the security contract, but not China in any way[15]. Pakistan was said not to be hostile to or guilty of violence against China[16]. This has expressed the willingness of both countries to achieve peace and cordiality.

The conference in Bandung was a significant event that demonstrated China's global strategy. China has achieved diplomacy in a way that is recognised as the Bandung Spirit as the driving force of China. Zhou Enlai has been able and has encouraged the participant to include 'Five Principles of Peace' in the conference manifesto. The conference's image of China was 'prestigious and responsible power.' The spirits of the Bandung Conference were followed by China and a host of agreements were signed with different states. [17]Via its conference in Bandung, China aimed to work with the Third World to monitor the onslaught by the United States against expanding Chinese hegemony in the area and around the world. Though China was willing to help on many regional problems, the US were uncompromising and inflexible.

In the 1950s, there were partnerships for a decade. On the world map, new states had arisen and rivalry between the Cold War and the United States had forged relations with the new-born countries. Smaller States have partnerships with major powers that are the most relevant to their own security objectives and are weighing advantages and weaknesses. Others demand immunity and life guarantees, others bargain with the superior states reimbursement for their defence costs. For certain smaller nations, alliances will also have economic advantages. In the 1950s, China and India established friendly ties, and Pakistan and China stayed distant. India pursued a stance of non-alignment that China welcomed while the US-supported alliances prevent Pakistan from claiming neutrality.

Two separate positions in the coming years have affected Pakistan-China ties. First, Pakistan could pursue a normal neighbourly China policy, which could be affected by China's tendency for India and Pakistan's adherence to the western pact directed against China. China's tendency for India, as Pakistan, anticipated an Indian security challenge and its entry into the Anti-China Agreement had little critical effect on its ties. Secondly, in particular as a result of Indian-Pakistan animosity and Pakistan's coercive security forces, China has correctly evaluated Pakistan's role. [18]This enabled China to see clearly that Pakistan was not a part of west alliances to fight China but just to safeguard its own security with India. It is therefore no surprise that China did not seem to be pulsating in reaction to many proposals under geo-political pressure.

From 18 April to 24 April 1955, the Bandung Conference was conducted. 29 representatives from new-born Asian and African countries were present The conference was the first time that Pakistan and China will meet at the summit table. Zhao En Lai and Mohammad Ali Bogra met with each other and invited them to visit their respective countries. Hussain Shaheed Suhrawardy, Prime Minister of Pakistan, visited China from 18 to 29 October 1956. The Joint Declaration of 23 October stated that discussions between the two leaders emphasised that friendship between them must be strengthened, that there must be shared understanding and that business and cultural ties should be encouraged.

In the 1950s Pakistan-China ties witnessed the rude patch, apart from the doubts that were created by Pakistan's joining security alliances allegedly against the Soviet Union and China to control communist attacks. Prime Minister Hussain Shaheed Suhrawardy's declaration of international communism as a threat to the free world, China's map showing Pakistan as a territory of China, small borders on the Pakistan–China border, an invitation to Indian Prime Minister Nehru by President Ayuba Khan for joint defence and a vote in favour of a UN resolution condemning Chinese action in Tibet were examples of this. [19] The animosity of India and China and the vote of Pakistan for the entry of China to the UNGA marked the start of the two countries' cordial ties.

Indeed, it was the rivalry between India and China over the border conflict that promoted friendly relations between Pakistan and China. The starting point was launched as a unilateral decision, along with his advisers, that the expansion of the Indian boundary to McMahon line drawn by the British until dividing the subcontinent was to be intensified by the Indian Prime Minister Jawaher Lal Nehru. On 20 November 1950, the parliament also ratified the resolution. In India, too, troops were transferred to McMahon Line for annexation. This tactic for escalation excluded the negotiations and China realised that the doors were locked for negotiating territorial conflicts. On 20 October and 16 November 1962, China reacted by launching an assault. After defeating the résistance, the Chinese military retreated from their initial roles of their plans.

3.3 Phase of Reconciliation and Empathy (1962-1978)

The post-1962 Chinese war between India and Pakistan may be called an age of peace and empathy between China and Pakistan. Clearly, Chinese-Indian rivalry opened up the way to peaceful bilateral ties between Pakistan and China. In Pakistan-China, the worsening links between India and China had led to a proportionate change. In this period, Pakistan and China started to recognise and change their sails accordingly to future geo-political realities. The two countries were near together and established a clear sense of common economic and political priorities as a result of their emphasis on regional and international issues and their priority for socio-economic development. Since 1962, because of the territorial conflict between India and China, it has been necessary for Pakistan to tackle the border delimitation problem with China in order to prevent any confrontation.

A vital invention from the late 1950s was the Karakoram Highway (KKH) or Friendship Highway in China. Though Pakistan and China did not have warm ties at the start of this initiative, it has proved to be one of both countries' most important ventures. The huge scheme, which started officially in 1966 but the first analysis began in 1960. The plant was finished in two decades and opened to the general public in 1979. The project that claimed the lives of 400 to 500 Pakistanis, and between 80 and 200 Chinese, linked Abbottabad in Pakistan by Gilgit-Baltistan with Kashghar at Chinese Xinjiang, one per 1.5 kms. [20]In addition to gaining a political and logistic lead, the 1,300kilometre-old KKH was built to foster commercial relations and contact with the people between Pakistan and China. In the latter part of the dissertation more on this will be addressed.

For the United States. In a special cabinet meeting on 18 Novembrance 1960 it was also agreed that Pakistan could not continue the inflexible role it has been taking since it began to take on China and Russia. In addition, Pakistan agreed to promote the legitimate acceptance of China in UNGA. [21]Pakistan's support for China appeared an unwise choice, depending on the US for protection and economic aid. The US had certain geopolitical compulsions and it was not feasible for the US to do anything outside established limits. A indicator of warmth in Pakistan-China ties was generated by Pakistan's decision on Chinese UN membership.

As Indian and China ties deteriorated as a result of the Tibetan Uprise[22], Pakistan discovered a Chinese map showing several interesting passes in the Chinese territories of Pakistan. There were also reports of certain movements of Chinese soldiers. The rough mountainous landscape from Pakistan was not visited by Pakistan because of the inaccessible regions.

Any of the Chinese aircraft have violated Pakistani airspace. President Ayub Khan suggested on 23 October 1959 boundary negotiations to settle the issue to fix the problem. The region was part of Cashmir and because of the contentious nature of the matter, China has not been responding to the bid for some time because it did not want its rivalry with India to intensify further.

Indeed, China's inability to resolve the border conflict with Pakistan has been certain. It was attributed to the political and diplomatic tendency of Pakistan. Pakistan responded cautiously to foreign and regional problems at the beginning of the 1960s. Pakistan proposed offering India a mutual defence pact, in the light of Indian conflict with China over the border dispute and skirmishes between the two countries. The reticence of Pakistan to the USA and the West and the careful approach to One China strategy has contributed to the hesitation of China. The Chinese ambassador, who called the plan a complicated problem, conveyed this to President Ayub Khan.

The Chinese leadership adopted this as a good move after Pakistan's vote on China in the UN in December 1961. Bilateral ties have been improved as well. As a constructive change on Pakistan's part, China received it. Foreign Minister Manzoor Qadir from Pakistan played a role in the negotiations with China on Pakistan's border conflict proposal. On 3 May 1962, the two governments announced their diplomatic attempts in order to settle the conflict. Pakistan and China concluded a boundary separation pact on 2 March 1963 (see Appendix A). The agreement will also be regarded as an interim arrangement, and the agreement will be supplemented by the sovereign authority in the region in the resolution of the Cashmir issue[23].

The Pakistan-India war of 1965 was the second war from the beginning. The first was over Kashmir in 1948, and the Karachi agreement was concluded. The war was followed by two major events. First, India-China territorial rivalry led to a war between India and China, and China emerged triumphant. The US and Western forces were shocked at India's vulnerability and its success in dealing with the communist attack that the West wanted to control. They also agreed, of equal importance, to evaluate the need for India to address the problem. Second, Pakistan has signed a border deal with China to put an end to all the concerns that have arisen in this matter. The US was wary of Pakistan's inclination by this deal. While some of the US did back the Cashmir conflict, India did have some control over Washington's political circles. It was difficult for the US to see that the

United States was supplying weaponry closer to communist China.

Kashmir was the great trigger of the war in 1965 and was left unfinished for the division in 1946, among a host of other causes. The Kashmir crisis was the culmination of three causes – Pakistan's religious nationalism, Indian nationalism and Kashmir's ethno-nationalism, according to Indian scholar Ashutosh Varshney. The topic has been haunted by many inconsistencies and paradoxes. [24] Negotiations between India and Pakistan have not progressed and the two countries have gone to war. Cashmir was kept up for an insurgency by the fighting that followed infiltrations of about 7,000 Indians[25]. And after the war, the condition quo which existed before the war persisted.

In the early mornings of September 6, 1965, the Skirmishes began in August 1965, and India attacked them. China was forthcoming and aggressive in supporting Pakistan among all of Pakistan's allies and friends. China supported Pakistan with unequalled assistance, warning India of severe damage to Pakistan's territorial integrity.[26] The assistance of China was notable in that it stopped large forces from siding explicitly with India. China considered India to be an aggressor and backed the right to self-determination in Kashmir. It was supported on 4 September 1965 by Chinese foreign minister Chen Yi. Yi reaffirmed that in compliance with UN resolutions and the aspirations of the Cashemiri citizens the matter of Cashmere should be addressed. This demonstrated China's deep support for Pakistan's Kashmir status. It also demonstrated China's failure to settle Kashmir's conflict conflict. Instead, China needed peaceful solutions to the Cashmir problem. Before the Indo-Pakistan war in September 1965, this was China's official stance.

Pakistan had joined the Western supported coalition before the Indo-Pakistan war in 1965, though India supported nonalignment. Meanwhile, only small assistance from Indonesia, Iran, Turkey and Saudi Arabia has been given to Pakistan. However, China endorsed the stance of Pakistan, and Chinese Prime Minister Zhou Enlai named India as an aggressor on 9 September 1965. China's involvement was apprehensive but was not done because of technical reasons and the threat of China against intervention and expansion of the dispute from the US and the Soviet Union. [27]In the 1965 conflict, China joined Pakistan in defiance of foreign pressures.

Pakistan faced an existential crisis in the early 1970s. The people of East Pakistan felt a sense of injustice and resentment about the policies of the country. In the late 1960s and early 1970s, this frustration became clear.

Many more questions arose during the National Assembly and Provincial Assemblies elections conducted on 7 and 17 December 1970. The problems raises before the polls often looked unworkable to the division and unity of policies.[28]The main issues were demand for regional sovereignty that almost implied dividing and using the wealth of East Pakistan through Western Pakistan.[29] This led to Pakistan's dismemberment.

The civil war between Pakistan's eastern and western wings and the continued Cashmir struggle between India and Pakistan contributed to Indo-Pakistan war in 1971. In response to alleged exploitation, the controlled West Pakistan establishment, extreme Bengali nationalism was brought to the fore. In an effort to bring an end to the revolt, a military campaign began on 25 March 1971 and the main objective is separatist Bengalis.[30]Sheik Mujibur Rehman was arrested, who had been elected to a plurality of seats at the general elections. Mass shootings and relocation have taken place as a result of the operation.

Following an evaluation of the crisis, Pakistan called on the United Nations to intervene. On 4 December 1971 a UNSC conference took place. The United States moved a motion for immediate cessation and retirement, but the Soviet Union rejected it and abstained the UK and France. On 12 December 1971, on the order of the United States, UNSC was called again, and a discussion on cessation of the fire began. Meanwhile, Pakistan's army gave in and the war ended. The U.S. and China backed Pakistan in the fight, while the Soviet Union and India supported Bangladesh's demand for freedom.[31] India supported Mukti Bahini by plans. Pakistan was to be dismembered. The United States was also worried that the area would become more and more Soviet.

Bangladesh has been a mixed response. On 25 January 1972 and 8 April 1972, it was acknowledged by both the Soviet Union and the US. China responded calmly to the crisis and put an effective cease-fire behind it. The report also revoked Bangladesh's appeal for membership in the United Nations and the non-implementation of a resolution on the repatriation of Pakistani citizens and prisoners of war. 1971 South Asian politics has been transformed by the India-Pakistan conflict. The conflict was complicated and the main actors of the Cold War were concerned. India decided to bleed Pakistan on the Kashmir issue because of its unchanging status.

The first nuclear bomb in Pokhran in Rajasthan was successfully tested on 18th May 1974. It has been called a peaceful nuclear explosion by the Indian Foreign Office, though independent analysts say it was part of India's concerted attempt to develop into a nuclear weapon. The first nuclear weapons attempt by a country other than the five permanent UNSC participants was a Pokhran nuclear test blast. Pakistan and China opposed the blast, which would trigger rivalry in South Asia and harm regional peace and stability. Pakistan's Prime Minister, Zulfiqar Ali Bhutto, replied by pointing out that it would never yield to a nuclear blackmai and would not take Indian influence in the region[32]284. A Nuclear Supplier Group was formed to control proliferation soon after an accident. In the dissertation elsewhere, this topic was addressed.

Reform and the opening up of China was another trend with regional and global ramifications. In December 1978, Deng Xiaoping led reformers introduced 'reform and initiation,‚ called 'Chinese socialism.'285 The changes were implemented in two stages. The reforms were implemented. The first step was to decollectivize farming and free up international investment and enterprises to companies. In the second step, state sector privatisation, protectionist measures and legislation have been implemented. As a consequence, there has been phenomenal private sector production and annual growth of almost 9 percent. The reforms also given not only economic dividends, but also Chinese culture shifts. This topic was explored in the dissertation on the growth of China.

3.4Phase of Friendship and Cordiality (1979-1990)

Four main domestic and regional growth enabled Pakistan-China ties to reach a new phase of cooperation marked the phase of friendship and cordiality. The reforms of China and opening up of the country were major progress in the process, the Soviet invasion of Afghanistan, the Tiananmen Square Incident in 1989 and the dismemberment of the Soviet Union. This has influenced both regional and international affairs. In addition to helping China enjoy its soft image worldwide, China's drive to implement structural reforms and open-up has also given economic dividends. On 24 December 1979 again, Soviet Union attacked Afghanistan, and the subsequent developments became a major step of the Cold War. During the Afghan War, both Pakistan and China operated together and had a good impact on their ties. China was in a poor light in the 1989 Tiananmen Square crisis, with Soviet dismemberment changing the direction of regional and global politics. The impact of these developments on Pakistan-China ties was important.

Reforms and openings pioneered by Deng Xiaoping and his fellow reformers have progressively persisted. Due to changes, government controls on industry decreased significantly and private-sector flexibility increased significantly, thereby enhancing economic growth. Deng's reform policy was evidently appreciative of the Radical Communist Party leaders who rejected the changes, but Deng stood steadfast and went ahead with his strategy Thanks to inefficient state economic system, problems developed and the state suffered severe losses. As a consequence, inflation increased sharply and in 1985 and 1988 became a concern. Nonetheless, during this time China has continued to expand significantly. In addition, thanks to changes, China started seeing privacy as a "supplement" to the public sector and then as a "significant part" of the state's fiscal system.[33]___

Another big trend of the Cold War was the Soviet invasion of Afghanistan. It had a significant effect on the ties between Pakistan and China. The war went on for about a decade from December 1979 and brought about permanent shifts in international and global affairs. The Soviet-Afghan war was an example of Cold War rivalries and a struggle for super-power. The war devastated the Soviet Union, when 14,454 men were killed, 50,000 injured and the expense of the war increased to $96 billion.[34]___ Afghanistan lost a great deal more, though. In Afghanistan, more than 870,000 Afghan citizens died, almost three million people were injured or maimed, one million people were displaced and over 5 million Afghan refugees fled to Pakistan, Iran and other asylum applicant countries.[35]___The Soviet-Afghan war was a major event where the Soviet Union demonstrated its expansionist concepts and the US employed both its military and diplomatic strength to monitor the Soviet Union's communist agenda.

In December 1979, the Soviet invasion of Afghanistan was the world's shock. It had its troops in Afghanistan and started with several initiatives the sovietization movement in Afghanistan. It called on its consultants to oversee government departments in the civilian and military realms of Afghanistan to control decision-making. Shortly after the war, about 1500 Soviet advisors and almost 4000 military men served respectively for civil government and the armed forces. Soviet influence was vast and seemed as if the Soviet Union's organisations and departments had been reshaped according to the Soviet Union standard. Twenty three The rising against the Soviet Union in the 1980s didn't take long for a powerful opposition movement.

The 1980s was Afghan's decade of opposition to the Soviet Union, which had engaged almost 80,000 staff in maintaining Afghanistan's occupation. The Soviet forces and the ally of the Afghans were tackled by many rebel groups, who had assistance from the US, Pakistan and the Kingdom of Saudi Arabia (KSA). Two larger guerrilla groups, made up of moderates and fundamentalist, emerged by the end of 1981, and extreme warfare began to impose massive casualties on human and materiality. At the UNGA Emergency Special Session on Afghanistan, the issue was raised and debated, and a resolution calling for the removal of troops and for the support of humanitarian aid was adopted.

In February 1986, in his speech to the 27th Party Congress, the Soviet leader Michail Gorbachev named the Afghanistan crisis a bleeding wound and declared that the forces should be retreated to end the war in Afghanistan.[36] His declaration resulted in a ferocious fight to secure a rapid victory, and in 1985 the Soviet-Afghan dispute became the bloodiest year. The U.S. started supplying the rebel groups with rocket weapons in 1986 for Soviet gunship helicopters. Twenty-seven The leadership of Afghanistan was Mohammad Najibullah on 30 September 1987 and the peace agreement between the US, USSR, Afghanistan and Pakistan was concluded on 14 April 1988 and troop retirement started shortly afterwards. The Soviet Union declared on 15 February 1989 the removal from Afghanistan of its last soldier. The retirement of the Soviet Union was not peaceful in Afghanistan since ferocious civil war lasted until the 1990s. But China faced the threat of Tiananmen in 1989, when the Soviet Union was disengaging from Afghanistan.

While Pakistan-China was unaffected by the Tiananmen square event, it ramified China not only as far as domestic politics were concerned, but also as regards its global profile. This event was evidently an unfortunate occurrence for China and marked China's stature as a society. When the citizens came together to mourn the deposed former secretary-general of the group Hu Yaobang and spoke about his expulsion, the incident blew up. Three representative students, on 22 April 1989, called for the Great Hall of People to meet with Prime Minister Li Peng, but did not react. Classes were boycotted by angry pupils. The official People's Daily newspaper said on 26 April, handful of students are causing chaos to remove the communist party and overthrow the authorities of the republic.

The Soviet Union's dissolution signalled a change in world order and international policy and also affected ties between Pakistan and China. The close of an age was marked and another began. In 1917, by overthrowing the Russian Czar, the progressive Bolcheviks established the Soviet state. After Kerensky, Vladimir Lenin, who was a Marxist, was the Soviet leader.

Though it was seen as a genuinely democratic society, the Russian regime was essentially totalitarian and ruthless. By 1924, the State had totalitarian control of economics and industrial activities when Joseph Stalin took power. Stalin's one-party government, also after his death in 1953, persisted. Three hundred The objective of Soviet Union during this period was the Cold War, in which all the superpowers had taken part in an arms race and had become competitive to increase the world's dominance.

In March 1985, in the Soviet Union, Mikhail Gorbachev came to power. He was confronted with a sleepy economy and a government system which was not suitable for change. He implemented glasnost and perestroika strategies. Glasnost meant democratic transparency and was aimed at cleansing censorship, growing the omnipresence of secret police, welcoming government critiques by media, granting people rights, and encouraging non-communist political parties to conduct political activity and challenge elections. Perestroika meant a transformation economy designed to allow for private entrepreneurship programmes and promote international investment. [37]These changes were to become a long-term aspect of an economic system which resulting in food scarcity and other associated issues raising people's discontent.

Gorbachev promised to take measures to ensure the prosperity and economic viability of the Soviet Union. He wanted friendly ties with the United States and wished to emerge from arms races. He felt the retreat of forces from Afghanistan was sufficient and the intervention there in Eastern Europe was significantly reduced. The Soviet hold on Eastern Europe was broken by his tilt towards non-intervention. A revolt sparked in eastern Europe with Poland taking the lead. This affected the Soviet Union, Estonia, Latvia and Lithuania, and the break-up of Belarus and Ukraine with the Soviet Union declared independence. The rest of the eight republics adopted a suit and the Soviet Union was declared to have disintegrated. The political rivalry between two superpowers in the area after the Second World War came to a close.

As Pakistan-China ties are discussed, the influence of numerous worldwide, international, and national trends since the Second World War needs to be analysed. The period of civil and military upheavals was between 1949 and 1990. In this area of the world the superpower competition was apparent as the Soviet Union, which is one of the bi-polar forces, was located near South Asia. The States were affected by the super power struggle. Pakistan has long been on the wrong side of Soviet Union when it opted to be part of US-backed partnerships that are constrained by their own armed forces. China also favoured the West alignment with Pakistan and several other foreign policy efforts. China felt uncomfortable.

A maritime transition has taken place on the world stage and both Pakistan and China like the US, former Soviet Union and other countries, in a two-way, regional and global sense, have had to adapt to the evolving and demanding times. In reality, after the Cold War, the time created new problems and possibilities, leading to the search for greener grasslands elsewhere and also maximise the advantages of their bilateral relationships. In parallel, the need to deal with both Pakistan and China has increased.

[1] Michael D. Swaine, "China: The Influence of History"

[2] Ibid

[3] "OECD Economic Surveys - China - 2015"

[4] "Cao Dawei and Yanjing Sun, China's History"

[5] " B. R. Ambedkar, Pakistan or the Partition of India. 1945"

[6] "Ebrey and Liu, The Cambridge Illustrated History of China"

[7] M. Akram Zaki, "China of Today and Tomorrow: Dynamics of Relations with Pakistan,"

[8] Rizwan Naseer and Musarat Amin, "Sino-Pakistan Relations: A Natural Alliance against Common Threats"

[9] K. Arif, China Pakistan Relations, 1947-1980

[10] Ibid.

[11] Melvyn P. Leffler and David S. Painter " Origins of the Cold War"

[12] Zaki, "China of Today and Tomorrow."

[13] Praveen K. Chaudhry and Marta Vanduzer-Snow, "The United States and India: A History Through Archives"

[14] Chandra Chari, Superpower Rivalry and Conflict " The Long Shadow of the Cold War on the 21st Century"

[15] "K. Arif, China Pakistan Relations, 1947-1980"

[16] "W. M. Dobell, "Ramifications of the China-Pakistan Border Treaty,"

[17] Denny Roy, "China's Foreign Relations"

[18] Pervaiz Iqbal Cheema, "Significance of Pakistan-China Border Agreement of 1963,"

[19] Arif, China Pakistan Relations, 1947-1980,

[20] Sarina Singh, "Pakistan and the Karakoram Highway"

[21] 2Arif, "China Pakistan Relations, 1947-1980"

[22] "Tibetan Uprising of 1959 referred to the rebellion that began in the capital of Tibet, Lhasa. A conflict that started between Tibetan rebels

and Chinese army in 1956 in Kham and Amdo regions intensified in March 1959. The guerilla war continued till 1962".

[23] "The Boundary Agreement Between China And Pakistan, 1963" March 2, 1963

[24] Ashutosh Varshney, "India, Pakistan, and Kashmir: Antinomies of Nationalism,"

[25] Ibid,1012.

[26] Naseer and Amin, "Sino-Pakistan Relations,".

[27] Panagiotis Dimitrakis, "Failed Alliances of the Cold War: Britain's Strategy and Ambitions in Asia and the Middle East"

[28] Dr Hassan Askari Rizvi, "First 10 General Elections of Pakistan"

[29] Ibid.

[30] Srinath Raghavan, 1971: A Global History of the Creation of Bangladesh

[31] Drong Andrio, "The Effects of Political Changes in the Relationship between Bangladesh and Russia (USSR) in 1971-2014"

[32] 3Arif, "China Pakistan Relations, 1947-1980"

[33] Lan Cao, "Chinese Privatization: Between Plan and Market,"

[34] Azhar Javed Siddiqui and Khalid Manzoor Butt, "Afghanistan-Soviet Relations during the Cold War"

[35] Ashley Jackson, "The Cost of War: Afghan Experiences of Conflict, 1978-2009"

[36] Susanne Sternthal, "Unraveling the Soviet Union: Gorbachev's Change in World View."

[37] Peter J. Boettke and others, "Why Perestroika Failed"

CHAPTER IV

Major Areas of Cooperation between Sino–Pak Axis

4.1 Triangular relationship

Triangular ties have been identified as an interdependent relationship between the three States and a close strategic alliance. The traditional triangular ties are largely embedded among symmetrical forces while the modern triangular relation is between asymmetrical forces and defends each other against external attacks. It is best understood by three players as a competitive transaction game. However, the third is asymmetrical, and two very different groups possess the same power. The intermediate influence of both sides induces to make the third power strategically in order for various benefits to be achieved. The trilateral relations were created in China during 770 B.C. and in the Greek city-state 221 B.C, not a freshly coined term[1]. In the West some scholars contend that in the decade of foreign affairs the geopolitical tri-angularity remains a significant phenomenon. The three asymmetrical powers were independent ruling regimes during the Cold War and post-Cold War. The leading characters in the international arena during the Cold War era were China, the US, and Russia. The three alliances based entirely on territorial expansion and void policy. In the other hand, modern triangular relations emerged in the current era and are mostly kept in secondary levels worldwide and the coexistence of competition and competition are central features of this relationship. Similarly, in contrast with the old trilateral players, the triangular players are seldom involved and are not distressing to each other[2].

4.1.1 Triangular international relations theories

The theory of the strategic triangle was established by Dittmer and Gerald Segal during the Cold War. The triangular arrangement depends on the intertwined behavior of the three sovereign players. The three parties have such common objectives that have helped to establish the triangular relationship. One country played a crucial role, whilst the other two played a key role[3].

In discussions and analyses on political science and international policy across the world, the definition of "strategic triangle" is also commonly used. A three-player transactional game may be considered as a triangle. The pivot and the wings are often allies and sometimes enemies in the strategic triangle, but both the wings have a strong relationship with the pivot. U. R. Ghai (2007)[4] states that two countries function as wings in a triangular relationship, while the third acts as the pivot.

4.1.2 Other Theories of International Relation about Triangular Relationship

There are many hypotheses analyzed to investigate actions in the partnership between China and Pakistan and the US.

The Strategic Triangle of Dittmer

The definition of the strategic triangle did not exist previously in literature but some foreign scholars cited in their work the trilateral or triangular partnership between three nations, including Dittmer (1981), Goldstein and Freeman (1991) and Womack (2004). Based on the philosophical context through which the relationship between the three countries has been analysed, Lowell Dittmer introduced the idea of a "strategic triangle[6]." The scientific progress of the geopolitical triangle, in which the three countries had interdependence, was stressed by Goldstein and Freeman (1991.

Dittmer used the phrase "Strategic Triangle" to analyses the relationships between the U.S., China and URSSR during the Cold War period, especially following Nixon's visit to China. The strategic triangle "can be considered as a kind of transactional game between three teams" Dittmer. The Member States join into the contract in a diplomatic triangle in order to accomplish those goals which cannot be accomplished properly at domestic level. These aims involve the trade of products and services as well as intelligence, propaganda and spying. The inter-governmental exchange of advantages (positive) and prohibitions (negative) exchange as commerce and warfare differentiated him. It is a symmetrical and often asymmetrical relationship sometimes[7].

It is not appropriate for two players to be symmetrical forces in the strategic triangle, Dittmer notes. However, they also perform the same part and defend the third (Pivotal small power). In the Cold War the United States, for example, supplied Japan with defence and Cuba with the Soviet Union. According to Dittmer, the big power is not going to try to build ties with the asymmetric forces, but is trying to avoid the risk of the young person finding relations with some other power.

During the Cold War, the United States and the Soviet Union rivalled each other to hold China in their respective area of control, whilst the boundary struggles between China and the Soviet Union became an incentive for China to turn towards the United States. At the same, China-Pakistan and the United States of South Asia are another geopolitical triangle. The symmetric forces are China and the US, and Pakistan is asymmetrical. China and the US both fight for Pakistan, while Pakistan deftly reaps the subtle force strive for better stability in the face of India (Smith P. J., The China–Pakistan–U.S. Triangle: From the Cold War to the "War on Terror" 2011)[8]. In order to reduce the security challenge faced by India, Islamabad aligned to the United States during the Cold War and when US changed its stance in the eyes of India, Pakistan tilted towards China.

"Every actor worries that each other's two will align against each other. There is this anxiety for all three actors and it is strongly concerned for China and India, the two poorer State actors. Beijing and New Delhi took steps to counteract the other's alleged contact with the US. The ensuing fear brought a new tension to the "out-" power's ties with the United States as these measures were not effective. Reducing interstate connections to a triangle instead of a multi-sided polygon would unilaterally reduce the amount of considered national actors" (Garver, 2002, p. 16).

Goldstein and Freeman Three-Way Street in Strategic Triangle

The geopolitical triangle was further examined by Goldstein and Freeman in their research "Three-Way Street: Strategic Reciprocity in World Politics," in which they looked into how the three major powers (US, USSR, and China) cooperated with one another in the pre- and post-Cold War period through conflicting interests. They also noted the impact of Chinese action on the US–Soviet relationship's dynamic and asymmetrical ties. To interpret the actions of great powers, the writers used three foreign hypotheses[9].

"The three possible state behaviors posted by IR theorists were not proved by Goldstein and Freeman: bureaucratic routine (states behave according to their own interests, where we can identify Classical Realism); reciprocity (behavior of states are influenced by other states, we can identify authors from the Interdependence Theory); and, third, that states respond to rational expectations (states respond not to the influence of other states, but behave according to rational expectations where reciprocity is not immediately evident, and the problem is that empirical results are contradictory"[10].

Three philosophies underpin the triangular relationships and attitudes of nation states: classical realism, interdependence theory, and realistic standards. States act according to their own needs, according to classical practical theory, while states' behavior is conditioned by the behavior of other states, according to interdependence theory. The third principle proposes that states react to reasonable desires rather than the effect of other states where reciprocity is not instantly apparent.

According to Ana So Liz de Stange (2015)[11], these three hypotheses may be used to describe the US-USSR and China triangular partnership. During the Cold War, the two major powers (the US and the USSR) acted according to their respective interests, and both states established ties with other small countries to try to accomplish political and economic goals. If the asymmetric force (China) was acting under the control of great powers, for example, during the early stages of the Cold War, China was acting under the influence of the USSR, the breakup of the Beijing-Moscow alliance in the 1960s and 1970s prompted Beijing to formulate its own foreign policy against the US. Following the US-China summit, Beijing's foreign strategy was mostly favoured by Washington in order to protect their own interests against the expanding communism of the USSR.

According to the expectation principle, a state's action is determined by its movements and countermoves. This is expressed in US policy against South Asia, which forced the Soviet Union to change its policy in the same area. During the Cold War, the USSR's reactions were mostly based on US behavior, but they had reciprocal effect on US-China and Soviet-China ties (Goldstein and Freeman 1991). The fair expectation/rational option principle asserts that states act based on their own decisions rather than being influenced by others. In his post, Ana So Liz de Stange describes that in triangular relationships, each state has their own set of choices on how to behave in the partnership. During the Cold War, all three nations (the United States, the Soviet Union, and China) acted rationally. The three players' policies were not intertwined, but their movements and countermoves were focused on their logical choices.

"The authors have found that, with regard to triangular encounters, "The effects of these simulations are harder to read as far as triangular answers are concerned. They briefly say that Chinese-Soviet conduct is triangular rather than the US behavior: The Soviet and Chinese regularly take the US behavior on board in their attitudes against each other"[12]."

The theory of asymmetric and triangles: Womack

In 2004, Womack proposed the principle of asymmetry and an Asymmetry triangle, arguing that during the Cold War, the diplomatic structure was multipolar dependent on the Chinese-Soviet Union-US military triangle. Womack also argued that, with the introduction of the two more countries (Japan and England), the multipolar structure of international post-Cold War extended and a stable matrix of an international system witnessed power asymmetries[13] (Stange, 2015).

Robert Joseph (2011), in part, discussed the "three asymmetric triangles," in which the author attempts to describe the total asymmetry of the relationship in triangles in his study published in Baylor University. The first kind of triangular connection consists of the symmetrical form, which has equivalent control in all three states. By means of this model, Womack has tried, in political, military and economic fields, to analysis the trilateral arrangements. The second form of strategic triangular asymmetric partnership involves the 'Twin-head Dual Asymmetric Triangle' in which all States are equal in strength and the third is asymmetrical. The US and China, for example, have the relatively similar political power which overshadow Moscow greatly. At the same time, the US and China and the Soviet Union have good connections and the three-way partnership has not been affected. The last paradigm for interactions is the Single-headed Dual Asymmetric Triangle, in which a state's strength far outperforms the power of the other two members[14] .

In 1982 Gerald Segal & Dittmer considered the development of ties between three nations as an inseparable whole from the viewpoint of the geopolitical triangle. It means that either as a result or as an outcome of handling interactions with the third actor or as a consequence, each of the three actors takes a specific decision in relation to the second actor.

International affairs and moral philosophy thinkers, such as Plato and Aristotle, also established a political science definition of idealism. The idealism principle is derived more from Socrates from Greek thinkers. Since then, the States also established relationships with their national interests with each other. Following that, with the rise of realism, the modern age of foreign affairs started. The founding father of the modern philosophy of realism was Hans Morgenthau. He dismissed the idealistic concept of foreign relations, and claimed that fighting the power was the core interests of states. his novel, Policy among Nations, has important implications on international relations philosophy. The philosophies of foreign affairs, such as realism and power balance, have emphasised the national objectives and behaviour. This perspective was supported by realistic teachers such as Machiavelli, Reinhold, and Hans Morgenthau. They highlighted the self-interest and passions of nations (International politics). They emphasised that the evolution of human existence was clear and that, by its very nature, man is selfish and has done all to achieve supremacy and superiority[15].

Another community of academics such as Kenneth Thompson, Thomas Hobbes, Machiavelli, E, H. Carr and Kenneth Waltz talk about reasons other than the drive to be able. But a significant focus was put on human behaviour and influence in their respective works. The thinkers stated above that gaining national influence is not the only part of foreign relations. Kenneth Thompson also argues that "man is a spiritual being in his bones" and stresses fairness. Machiavelli is a realistic scholar, but he should not hesitate to acknowledge that they are malicious (The Prince). Thomas Hobbes believes, even at the cost of their own interests, that idealism functions for the benefits of the others. Hobbes contributes to some of the fundamental concepts in international relations, particularly neorealism, of realistic traditions. He says that the idea of world chaos is egoistic toward human existence. Hobbes is the chief advocate of the power battle. Through the passing of time, Carr's state realism shifts his form. Carr's critics criticise Morgenthau that moralism is not the rational effect of realism that depends rather on the failure of another nation state'sachievement[16]. [17]Thompson (1966) says that because classical antiquities and the individual's existence is selfish, human nature has not improved. Just the selfish desires of nations inspire him.

The practical international school creates the idea of polarity in international affairs. The Poles played a major part in the internationally, the logical thinkers claim. The States alliances are together to safeguard their respective regional rights. This led to a revolution in foreign affairs' balance of force. Four main elements that define the role of a polar force in the international system are described in the realist school of thinking. The following flowchart shows certain components[18].

4.2 Pakistan-China Economic Dimensions

While security cooperation was exceptional, Pakistan-China ties also showed a sufficiently large economic dimension. Again, though relations with China commenced in the late 1950s when diplomatic relations began, the economic relations between the two countries became dynamic with the granting to each other of the Most Favorite Nation (MFN) title. A

Blueprint was later provided for in trade ties by the Trade Agreement concluded in 1963. The Joint Committee on Economy, Trade and Technology between Pakistan and China was formed in 1982.[19]The FTA was concluded in 2006 with a view to speeding up bilateral exchange. By 2013, China was the second-largest trading partner in Pakistan. In 2015, when they decided to launch the multi-dimensional CPEC programme, both countries made a quantum leap. Pakistan and China would therefore concentrate their economic ties in the post-Cold War period on commerce, investment, electricity and infrastructure.

As former Ambassador Masood Khan said, Pakistan-China business ties have thrived on a supportive atmosphere where both countries have shared on regional and international matters. Trade and economic ties remained a top priority of any bi-lateral partnership with China and Pakistan during their high-level visits to each other's country with a well-defined roadmap.[20] The 2014-15 trade figures pointed to that with an 18.2 per cent rise in trade between Pakistan and China. This rise in bilateral trade was seen during the first three months of 2016 and a growth of 10 percent (4.4 billion dollars) was seen.[21]However, China stood in control of the balance of trade, as Pakistan's trade sector failed to grow its infrastructure.

The wheat, corn, hides and skins, chemical material, fish and crude oil were the most important exports Pakistan made to China. The biggest Chinese imports were machines of all sorts and pieces, clothing, textile products, stationary objects, building materials, vaults and sanitary goods and rubber pipes.[22]In the decade 2000-2010, there was a real joy in trade ties between the nations. In November 2002, the Preferential Trade Agreement (PTA), with the objective of providing tariff advantages for different goods, was signed by Pakistan and China. Free trade negotiations started in 2005, and in November 2006, an FTA deal was eventually concluded. In July 2007, the FTA was ratified.[23]According to the deal, Pakistan has held no duties on such goods, while China has cut its tariff to 50% for knit and tissue. From 2007 to 2011, exports from Pakistan to China increased 33% and imports increased by 9% a year. In 2007–2008, however, China continued to support Pakistan's trade deficit and increased from $2,34 billion to $2,5 billion in 2010–11[24].

In 1978, China made a political decision in the context of the reforms to cultivate good neighbourly ties for sustainable economic growth. Pakistan cannot take complete economic benefit of its strong ties with China, despite being closely related to other countries in the area. The economic ties with China were seen as lax by the Pakistani business community. With shipments to China up by 400 per cent in a decade, China's trade rate remained greater. For example, in 2014 China exported $9.3 billion in products to Pakistan and $2.62 trillion to China could be exported to Pakistan. This illustrates clearly that the Free Commerce Agreement was not able to make good use of Pakistan.[25]Pakistan did not use a waiver it had under the Chinese Pacific Free Trade Agreement (CPFTA), and just 3.3% of tariff lines, according to the Ministry of Commerce analysis. The ministry analysis revealed that Pakistan may export 253 of China's 7550 total tariff lines. There were tariff talks between Chinese officials and Pakistani business leaders on different issues.[26]Yet FTA's advantage was in China's favor.

A report carried out in 2013 by the Pakistan Business Council described numerous difficulties faced by the ties between Pakistan and China following the signing of the FTA. Pakistan and China initially planned to reach $15 billion in bilateral exchange. However, because of systemic causes, the bilateral exchange rose from 2.8 billion dollars in 2005 to 9.3 billion dollars in 2012. Instead, trade between India and China has grown from 17 billion to 68 billion dollars, with the goal of raising it to 100 billion dollars.[27]Phase I of the FTA was completed in December 2012. Phase II negotiations started in July 2013 and since then, the two parties have held six meetings without a resolution on preferential concessions. [28]The FTA's Phase I trade balance was strongly weighted to favor China, which led to Pakistan wanting to apply the unilateral tariff system under FTA II to Pakistan. Initially China accepted but subsequently rejected its commitment and instead requested Pakistan to continue liberalizing its tariff regime to 90%.[29]Pakistan has provided just half of the total product line for the second stage of FTA to remove duties as the Pakistani industry was impacted by the dumping of cheap Chinese goods[30].

Pakistan will hardly draw remarkable numbers even in terms of investment. In 2000 FDI in Pakistan was USD 322 million, up to USD 5,4 billion in 2008, down to USD 3,7 billion in 2009, and USD 1,7 billion in 2011. FDI is currently in the middle of 2012. FDI spending was larger in the United States, the UAE, Switzerland and the United Kingdom. China's FDI share amounted to 0.5% but rose in 2006-2007 to 14% in 2006-2007. [31]After the CPEC deal, there was a noticeable shift in Chinese investment in Pakistan. The share of Chinese investment was tiny even during 2000-2005 with Pakistan's investment increasing by 600 per cent, amounting in 2004-2005 to 400,000 dollars. In 2006-2007, China was first among Pakistan's top three investors. In 2013, Chinese investment was between $5 billion and $7 billion, according to informal estimates.[32] In 2008, at the time of Pakistan's failure, China rejected the bailout programme, requested by then President Asif Ali Zardari during his official visit, to save the nation from the financial crisis[33].

As regards funding and expenditure, China started to support Pakistan in the early 1960s. There were few joint ventures launched in Pakistan by China in the fields of energy, infrastructure development and heavy machinery: Heavy mechanical Complex, Karakoram Highway, Gwadar Deep Sea Port, Chashma, Karachi Nuclear Power Plant (KANUPP), Indus Highway, Saindak Metal Project and Macran Costa Highway[34]

China re-ejusted its political as well as economic paradigm during the post-Cold War era, reflecting the evolving situation in which China became quickly a major player. China opened its doors to global trade in the 1990s not only for growth and prosperity, but also revived global ties to establish new friendships and alliances. The motto of 'constructive interaction' was appropriately lifted by President Xi Jinping so as to bring its purpose to the world. [35]In line with the geopolitical goals of China, it actively forged alliance and collaboration, which led to an increase in trade between both countries In 2105 CPEC was established by enhanced collaboration.

Xi Jinping's concept of the Seed Road in Kazakhstan was proposed in 2013 with the goal of building stronger relations with the Euro-Asian zone in his quest for a positive commitment throughout the world. In early 2015, China proposed the contours that will cross Central, South Eastern and South Asia of the Silk Road Economic Belt. The one-Belt One Road (OBOR) will also serve as an opportunity to promote trade collaboration and cultural exchanges on Silk Road and 21st century Maritime Silk Road.

Here, it may be important to examine why China's investment in a world experiencing security problems has been unparalleled. There are three explanations for China's outstanding sponsorship of Pakistan, according to Louis Ritzinger. Firstly, when the US shifted its attention to India, China needed to provide economic assistance to a long-standing ally in the area to curb China's growing presence in the region. Secondly, China has been involved in a Middle East oil trading path. Third, by linking it with the Middle East, Africa and Europe, Pakistan will allow China to achieve its global ambitions. [36]It would show that CPEC is a key pillar of the vision of the OBOR in China.

From the viewpoint of China, it will also extend Chinese regional and global reach, in addition to capturing huge economic dividends by making it accessible for the Indian Ocean and allowing it maritime links to the locked countries of West Asia and Central Asia. With regard to Pakistan, connectivity through various regions at the Gwadar harbour will enhance the strategic significance of Pakistan. CPEC will also benefit from Iran, Afghanistan, India and Central Asia, along with rising their economic stakes. The disparity between the neighbouring countries including India and Pakistan is likely to be settled in this new process.

The 'One Belt, three Passages, Two Axes, Five working zones' will be given by the CPEC.[37] A belt consisted of a strip shaped from Kashgar to Islamabad to Lahore to Sukkur that ends in Karachi and Gwadar. The Belt constituted the central CPEC regions. Three traffic passageways from Islamabad to Karakhi and Gwadar related to the east, centre and west. The key corridor roadway, the eastern passage, run from Islamabad via Lahore to Karachi. Multan, Sukkur, Haiderabad and Faisalabad. The main crossing started in the north of Islamabad and reached Karachi via Darya Khan, Jacobabad, Khuzdar via N25 and the Gwadar via M8. The western passage begins in Islamabad and passes through Dera Ismail Khan, Quette, Basima and Hoshab to Gwadar. Two axis, e.g., Lahore-Islamabad-Peshawar and Karachi-Gwadar axes were developed to organise development for regions. CPEC has also included five functional areas based on production, resource capabilities, market structure and growth potential.[38] At Gwadar, the centre of CPEC, all the routes converge.

The ongoing Indian-Pakistan conflict has posed the external security threat. The broad opinion was that the Indian intelligence services had sponsored the rebellion to sabotage CPEC in Balochistan. India was concerned that China's ongoing and steady involvement in Gwadar would enhance its strategic importance in the area and provide quick access to the Indian Ocean for the Chinese navy. India was angry with Gilgit-baltistan and Pakistan on the CPEC route, and Kashmir was held in Pakistan, which are territories that India considers contested.[39] In India, not just the Baloch separatists but also their world leaders have been in touch.[40] During Pakistan's Parliamentary Committee briefing, Lieutenant General (Retired), Pakistian Defense Secretary AlamChattak, said that a special cell, with an enormous amount, had been formed in Delhi by the Indian Research and Analysis Wing (RAW) to sabotage the CPEC Project. RAW also has been reputed to have worked closely with the Afghan intelligence service, the

National Directorate for Security (NDS). [41] However, the spirit of CPEC could not be dampened by internal problems and external threats and conspiracies, and the project started with trust and pace.

As part of the CPEC initiative, on 31 October 2016 Pakistan and China starts their first trade operation. The Susat Port, Hunza crossed more than a hundred Chinese trading containers. Susat was Pakistan's last city, off China's frontier on the Karakoram highway.[42] The first shipment of Chinese products rolled off the port of Gwadar on 13 November 2016 as a landmark incident. [43] The CPEC will create 700 000 direct employments between 2015-2030, according to US-based consultation company Deloitte and Touche. As a consequence of the CPEC, the growth in economic activity was forecast to increase GDP from 5% to 7.5%. It will greatly support the cement, construction and transport industries.[44] CPEC will transform Pakistan's lifestyle and not only deliver economic benefits but promise a change in perspective and way of thought for them.

The benefits of the CPEC will, as discussed earlier, spread through the whole area and play a key role in achieving peace and stability through economic stakes. For example, India might build on the Middle Eastern and Central Asian connectivity infrastructure of the CPEC.

The Iran-Pakistan-India pipeline under the CPEC was another opportunity. This will not only have the funds needed, but also solve the geopolitical problems that required India to be removed from the pipeline. Similarly, the railway project for China's Iran could also improve communication between India and Iran. [45]If we take advantage of this new model of economic connectivity, the long-standing problems concerning ties between India and Pakistan will have the opportunity to be amicably resolved.

It is also no surprise that President Hassan Rouhani of Iran is keen to enter the CPEC. For over a decade, Iran has been economically isolated by US sanctions. Now, the government strives to dilute the impacts of long-lasting trade restrictions in the outside world. Iran's natural instinct was to link up with its natural friends in the vicinity of the CPEC. Iran is currently trading with China through Central Asian states, increasing the cost of manufacturing Iranian products and services. Gwadar's Port is a natural transit for Iran to deliver its products across the Indian Ocean just one hundred kilometres from Iran. The world's 10% oil reserves were available in Iran. [46]Iran could double its oil exports to China and other countries both within and across the country by an alternate path.

In 1963 Pakistan established the Most Favored Nation (MFN) status of China, which led to economic links between Pakistan and China. Since then, not only have both countries cooperated together with each other but have strengthened economic and commercial ties. There have been consistent bilateral trade relations between China and Pakistan. While Pakistan did not get the most from this relationship due to numerous systemic deficiencies and contradictory financial and trade policies. There is substantial trade deficit between Pakistan and China, with imports from Pakistan from China at 9 billion dollars, while exports from Pakistan to China are at 2 billion dollars.

The CPEC has improved the economic relationship between Pakistan and China. This bilateral infrastructure project of 46 billion dollars was deemed a revolution in South Asian geopolitics. As a reaction to Pakistan's economic problems, the CPEC, a network of 3,000 kilometres of roads and other infrastructure was seen as almost incapacitating. In various energy-related ventures, China spends $34 billion. Of course, his concern is multifarious since this network will cut China's access by 12,000 kilometres to the Middle Eastern and African markets. The military naval power of Pakistan will rise significantly as China will provide Pakistan with eight CPEC submarines. Connectivity powered by the CPEC will put regional links where South and Central Asian nations profit from trade and investment opportunities in these countries together.

The diplomatic, geopolitical and economic ties of Pakistan-China will be detrimental to the idea that international relations had no enduring allies or enemies. The geopolitical position in Pakistan, with China's economic interest in the area and in Pakistan, was a significant factor in strengthening the relationship. China's joint hostilities against India became a key factor. There was some bitterness between Pakistan and China in the Cold War, when Pakistan was America's most reliable partner, which was quickly resolved. Pakistan-U.S. links became compromised immediately after the Cold War period, owing to Pakistan's attempts to achieve nuclear capabilities. Pakistan-China grew together during the same time and China sponsored Pakistan, as well as valuable diplomatic, military and economic ties.

From the outline above, it will be obvious that there is a kind of coherence in economic ties between Pakistan and China, which involve trade, investment, electricity and construction of infrastructure. In this respect, China has always been on the lookout to extend assistance of some sort. Due to the recent spate of investment in CPEC, the so-called Game Changer CPEC will push the economic relationship between China and Pakistan to a new height. In the three thousand-kilometer street that connects the Chinese province of Xinjiang to Pakistan and the port of Gwadar will be a huge investment of 46 billion US Dollars. Pakistan's greatest advantage from this relationship is that of the energy ventures proposed in various parts of Pakistan. This new investment transmitted a clear indication beyond Pakistan that Pakistan could not be labelled as terrorism. Pakistan's economic outlook changes with this new investment. The very fact that trade between Pakistan and Chine grew by 18.2 percent in the 2014-2015 fiscal year reveals a growing economic relationship between both countries.

4.3 Pakistan-China Strategic Dimensions

Chinese-Pakistan Strategic Ties have been built on a long-term, diplomatic, military, social and historical relationship.[47] In Pakistan-China ties, although the word strategic relations generally refers to collaboration in defence and security between two or more countries, the term may be used in bilateral relations even relating to education, health care, exchange and investment. This will help Pakistan strengthen its strategical capability in the field of security and defence by discussing infrastructure growth. The economics, which was necessary to promote a nation's strategic building, also consolidated its development infrastructure.

In the early 1960's, safety was the principal 'stimulus' for developing ties between China and Pakistan that later grew into diplomatic, economic and strategic dimensions.[48] Two developments, the border dispute between India and China in 1962 and the Indian-Pakistan war in 1965, dramatically changed both countries' geopolitical perspective. Security issues also highlighted each meeting between the two countries in time of peace and conflict. Foreign policy in Pakistan has particularly established China's position in the security field and China has reciprocated the development of the missile system and military and defence facilities by equipping Pakistan with experteny and technology.

Since diplomatic ties had been established in the early 1950s, traditional and unorthodox cooperation between Pakistan and China existed. Pakistan entered Western Europe in the 1960s in order to satisfy the standard weapons demand. But Pakistan was compelled to search for other vendors and find China able to assist at high cost and small supplies. In 1962, China's 1959-Indian boundary war prompted Pakistan to supply its proximate ally in Southern Asia with traditional weaponry. Followed by interest-free advances of 60 million dollars and more than 40 million dollars in 1969. These lending aided Pakistan in the construction of heavy mechanical complexes. [49]China also provided a $300 million credit to Pakistan in 1972 to build its military and economic infrastructure[50] . It was the start of ties between China and Pakistan that lasted until today.

In the past, Pakistan's main suppliers of weapons and explosives had been America, Europe and China since the 1970s. Pakistan had been dependent on all these outlets for all of its three powers to obtain defence supplies. In the 1980s, the United States obtained fighter planes, helicopters, auto pistols, APCs, ship by ship and air lancers from the United States[51]. In the 1990's, Pakistan acquired Western countries' fighter jets, warships, warships and tanks.[52] Aircraft, tanks and surface-to-air missiles were, however, procured from China during the 1980s and 1990s, and the host of other defence equipment. [53]The West and the Soviet Union rejected Pakistan's sale of weapons in fear of alienating India.[54] Finally, China made Pakistan secretly and openly capable of expanding its defences in modern lines.

China helped Pakistan to develop defense-related infrastructures, in particular Pakistan POF (Protective Ordinance Factories) and the Heavy Industries Taxila (HIT). China assisted Pakistan in setting up Wah POF in the 1960s. There were 14 plants that produced different types of machinery, arms and clothes. All three facilities were manufactured by the factories. [55]The High Industries Taxila was first devoted to the reconstruction of Chinese T-59 tanks. The facility had five units for the rework, installation and manufacturing of the key combat fuel tank (MBT) and AST tanks of the Chinese T-series and of American M-series and the manufacture of weapons barrels. MBT-2000 or Al-Khalid was the indigenous manufacturing of HIT. 368 The Pakistan Aeronautical Complex began in 1999, with the aid of China, to construct JF-17 Thunder. This one-engine multi-roller jet improved Pakistan Air Force's capacity to engage outside visual range. China decided in 2015 to use the equipment it was selling in Pakistan to construct four of the eight submarines. [56] Both countries continued engaged in defence dialogues to address topics relating to military and defence relations in order to monitor and streamline strategic partnering.

Although the founder of nuclear co-operation between Pakistan and China was Pakistan's Prime Minister Zulfiqar Ali Bhutto (1972-1977), this collaboration persisted in the later years. In the 1980s and shortly after the

Cold War in the 1990's, the collaboration peaked. It could not be completely understood how China helped Pakistan to enable it attain its nuclear aspirations, but the US surveillance indicated that Pakistan's nuclear programme would not have been effective without active assistance from China. China has provided Pakistan with vital assistance for developing the arms programme. Pakistan was supposed to own seven to 12 nuclear warheads by the 1990's on the basis of Chinese architecture and technology. The US was obliged to enforce restrictions on many countries by nuclear ties.

The declining interest of US in Southern Asia, and particularly in Pakistan, was a driving force for closer military as well as political rapprochement of Pakistan and China. China came to Pakistan's assistance and offered defense technologies in the 1990's, when the US put Pressler's embargo on Pakistan to compel it to curb its nuclear program. In the 2011 Congressional Research Center study, China moved ring magnets for uranium enrichment to Pakistan between 1994 and 1995. In her paper, Lisa Curtis, Senior Research Fellow at the Asian Study Centre, observed that China provided Pakistan with technologies and technical resources to help it develop its nuclear program.[57] In his paper in India Review, General Banerjee went much further and said that China enabled Pakistan not only to develop its nuclear arsenal, but also to perform the first nuclear test on China's soil in the 1980s. [58] Again, China, although through 'unwitting private suppliers,' was to become an important supplier of Pakistani nuclear and missile products. Indeed, China, facing foreign condemnation, was the only country to support Pakistan develop its defense and military capability.[59] In post-Cold War, China and Pakistan were taken ever together by America's conflict with Pakistan on nuclear issues.

However, China refused to admit publicly that it was supporting the Pakistani nuclear military programme and that it was supporting it.The silence on China's clandestine funding of Pakistan was first broken on 9 February 2015, when Wang Xiaotao, main representative at the National Commission of Development and Reform (NDRC), in a press brief, recognised that China had helped Pakistan construct six nuclear nuclear reactors and exported more quickly. The nuclear power plants had a total of 3.4 million kilowatts.[60] This information was rendered as voices were raised in the Nuclear Suppliers Group against this partnership (NSG).

Pakistan has developed many facilities indigenously to promote the military and nuclear programme, including: SPD Division, Pakistan Atomic

Energy Commission (PAEC), Khan Research Laboratories (KRL), NESCOM, and the Ministry of Defense Production (MODP). Pakistan's pursuit of its nuclear aspirations is characterised by the mere presence of such entities.[61] Although the US and India were uncomfortable with China-Pakistan nuclear cooperation, Chinese strategic assistance to Pakistan remained unchangeable[62].

Cooperation in defence has begun to increase between Pakistan and China. The cooperation included nuclear aid, conventional weapons purchases and joint operations, including military anti-terrorist training. Both countries have built an outstanding network at establishment level with increased institutional trust. Late, Gwadar Harbour, with a view to controlling the expansionist agenda for India, has expanded its opportunities for strategic naval cooperation with India and possibly undermining its Arab and Indian Seas impact[63].Pakistan's strategic ties with China will surely continue to improve with this new growth.

There was another aspect of the ties between China and Pakistan, where Pakistan allowed China to provide access to Western military technologies that enabled Beijing scientists to perform reverse engineering. The US had tacitly allowed clandestine technological transfers to China during the Cold War to strengthen its ties with China. In 1982, the Central Intelligence Agency (CIA) threatened that the US would expect it to enter China if it sold the radar alarm device AN/ALR-69 into Pakistan as part of the F-16 Fighter Jet package. The selling was finally accepted.[64]China wanted Western technologies for aircraft to a large extent. In 1980, as the U.S. began to export F-16 Fighter Jet to Pakistan, China was particularly concerned about the latest equipment that could then be available only to the United States' closest ally. In 2011, after the US Seals raid in Abbottabad killing Osama bin Laden, the biggest access was given. The American intelligence authorities tasked Spy Agencies Pakistan with providing the skin of the downed Hawk, containing stealth equipment[65]. This continued consolidation of ties between Pakistan and China.

In the aftermath of the cold war, China shifted its goals to its global commitments, as the geopolitical focus of the world changed. As a leading nation, China wished Pakistan a safe world that was as good as Pakistan.[66] Pakistan's strategic ties with China have developed into a common and persuasive strategic challenge to India. The Indian aspect was more significant than violence, because both countries were not in line with the order that the US considered fit for South Asia's vision. [67] The strategic relations between Pakistan and China have taken five decades. In the geopolitical calculus Pakistan-China, India was the focus due to the various outstanding problems with both countries. Pakistan-China strategic ties have been a 'reaction to India-US strategic partnership' in the shifting dimensions of regional and global politics, particularly after the cold war. [68]The sort of interaction between the US and China with Pakistan has always been a discrepancy. The US still took political benefit in terms of strategic ties with a strategic leverage, while China will want to depend on itself without intervention in Pakistan's domestic affairs. [69] China-Pakistan ties have continued to develop and continue to challenge foreign theory that there are no lasting political allies or enemies.

Strategic or military ties have taken the lead in all kinds of relations between China and Pakistan. Otherwise for China, Pakistan may not have established its nuclear capability as soon as possible. China provided a steady stream of conventional weapons, a large part of its ballistic missile programme and consistent diplomatic support over half one hundred years in Pakistan. The relationship with Pakistan in China started with military support when China provided Pakistan not only at lower rates for defence equipment, but also without any supply condition as the US or other western countries did. Following the cold war, Pakistan was literally left by the US with a number of penalties imposed on a country that was trying to become a nuclear power, the path in strategic relations between both countries followed it.

China's aid to Pakistan to become a nuclear power came more quickly as Pakistan's nuclear programme was primarily a reaction to the nuclear programme of India. Nevertheless, both Pakistan and China refused to enter into nuclear relations. Receiving these assertions was only recently made in 2015 by the Chinese officials. Pakistan-China further deepened relations with China, which provide arms from combat jets to guided missile combatants. With 47% of China's arms Exports to Pakistan, China has become China's largest weapons purchaser according to Stockholm International Peace Research Institute (SIPRI). The Indian and the US component is behind China's military and political support for Pakistan. India had assisted the US not only on the Arab Sea, but also as a participant in a civil nuclear agreement with the United States, in the containment policy of China. The CPEC events, defence cooperation and submarine construction in Karachi will tackle the Indian Maritime Challenge in the Indian Ocean and the Arab Sea.

4.3.1 Military Cooperation Sino-Pak

While in the beginning of the fifties the Chinese formed their first high-quality connections in Pakistan, the Sino-Indian- relations prevented the acquisition of a military component from the Sino-Pak partnership, However, China only started developing Pakistan after Sino-Indian ties were deteriorating in the wake of the 1962 Sino-Indian Conflict. The rise of India's defence powers in Western weapons assistance to India at the start of 1963 enabled Pakistan search for an alternate means of funding, because Pakistan had no longer had faith in the West. Pakistan stared anxiously at China, and Chinese determination to emphasise Pakistan's fear was a hectic liquor.In a delegation visiting Pakistan, Chinese Prime Minister Chou-en-lai said that China will protect Pakistan worldwide, as Pakistan defended China in CENTO and SEATO.He expressed strong support for the case of Pakistan on Kashmir during his visit to Pakistan in 1964. Previous neutrality was abandoned and the stance of Pakistan was endorsed. India and Pakistan had been asked to settle the issue bilaterally. China hoped that "the conflict in Kashmir would be settled in line with Indian and Pakistani wishes of Kashmir citizens."[70]Sino-Pakistan ties were deepened in March 1965 when President Ayub visited China.

It also seems certain that in the event India took some heavy military action against Pakistan the Chinese underwrote the defence of East Pakistan. On a note of solidarity for "the citizens of Pakistan to preserve their freedom and dignity," the People's Daily, Beijing, reaffirmed in a China commentary on Pakistan's sentence of infiltrators to Cashmir.[71] Following Pakistan's huge weapons assault on Chhamb across international boundaries on 1 September 1965, Chen Yi came and expressed Chinese full solidarity and encouragement for the "just battle of the Kashmirian people to withstand Indian tyranny" and strong support for "Pakistan's righteous action to condemn the protests of armed Indians." In a statement issued on 7 September, after the start of a counter-offensive by India, the Chinese Government "revealed Pakistan with complete assistance, in an attempt to beat back indian aggressors."[72]Chinese leaders defended Pakistan's 'just' cause and charged that, on orders from the imperialists of the ninety and revisionists, the U.S. and Russia, she was exposed to Indian violence, indicating that Pakistan was determined to have moral and material assistance. The Chinese even undermined the United Nations' position. In a writer's terms, "Anyway, Pakistan was not dishonoured with its blank cheque. Any amount we wrote on it (military equipment) was actually paid out Military ties between Pakistan and China, dated from 1965 to 1966, involve discussions on security issues, China's weapons supply to Pakistan and its support to improve the development of Pakistani indigenous defence. In 1965, China sold missiles and combat supplies against a background of Pakistan's weapons losses and, in particular, the US arms embargo. First arms were delivered to Pakistan in early 1966, and, as Pakistan's first acknowledgment of Chinese guns and vehicles, Chinese Mig-19 and T-59 tanks were added on March 23, 1966 in its Parade. After the Indo-Pak war of 1965 the US weapons embargo on the subcontinent was disappointing to Pakistan and they started to pursue direct military collaboration with the Chinese.

"During the War of 1965, the secret pact between Pakistan and China has been widely speculated. This enduring uncertainty was cleared somewhat when, during tensions, Bhutto revealed that he had gone to Beijing. During the Indo-Pak battle, he was able to obtain some armaments and a degree of Chinese support.[73] The result of the 1965 Indo-Pak war often worried China. Since China fears that the Super Powers will take advantage of some change in the region's balance of power and establish their footprint. Then it sent India an ultimatum to disassemble all military facilities at and across the border with China/Sikkim within three days or suffer serious repercussions in order to place pressure on India during the high tensions. It's never another issue if this danger materialised. There is however another point of view in which the Chinese ultimatum was aimed at the Pakistani government to decide whether or not the Chinese wished to go with it all. For one time, whether Pakistan would align itself with China, its irreversible alienation from the West and Pakistan would be changed into North Vietnam or North Korea. The effects were ready for China to face. The consequences were reflected by Pakistani politicians. In order to continue long-distance struggle, Pakistan must rely entirely on China for a thousand years, as Bhutto put it, and maybe had to transform its culture into similar lines. Furthermore, if the broad movement of the Chinese troops were to call for American action, major problems would emerge under the backdrop of Kashmir. Pakistan rejected the broader dispute, much to China's dismay. [74]It was the only nation that publicly condemned Pakistan's statement as a "dirty trick" and "joint US-Soviet collusion with China"[75], and that was dissatisfied with the US talks on India under Soviet auspices.

During the war of 1965, India did not target East Pakistan. There was also substantial suspicion during that period. There have been some unconfirmed claims that China, the United States and Pakistan have some kind of understanding to underpin East Pakistan's safety. The Tashkent agreement as a super power, particularly Soviet, was fiercely opposed by China, which characterised it as a 'dirty trick' and was highly unsatisfied with Pakistan's involvement in the agreement. He was not willing to admit face loss, but tried to interrupt the meeting. China proceeded to charge India and boundary provocation after the truce and held military momentum alive.

In its economic and internal security problems China had been cooperating steadily with Pakistan throughout the 1990s. As the Kargil war broke out between Pakistan and India in May 1999, China's diplomatic warning became obvious. During the Kargil Conflict, China demonstrated retention and requested all parties to pursue a diplomatic solution to the issue that was mutually decided upon. China demonstrated patience rather than lending Pakistan unlimited assistance like it did during the wars of 1965 and 1971. China opted for conciliatory action in order to avert regional unity arising from Pakistan's entry into Kargil. China's attitude to India has not changed much, despite the political transition.

China backed Pakistan's role in maintaining its constitutional right to share influence with India. In this spirit, China has always defied India's efforts to become a part of the group of nuclear suppliers (NSG). In response to India's efforts in building nuclear warheads utilising nuclear material provided by the USA and Canada, the coalition consisted of forty-eight nations.[76] In order to persuade international communities to allow India to join the NSG, US used their leverage. In 2008, the NSG granted an Indian exception authorising it to trade with different countries on nuclear weapons. India was however refused complete membership. China may have had its own motives for opposing India's inclusion in the NSG; Pakistan saw it as convergence of the interests of Pakistan and China.

The nuclear pact between the US and India in 2015 resulted from India's waiver at the 2008 NSG conference in Vienna. China saw the agreement as a possible counter-China step or containment and a modern Indo-US alliance variant.[77] India once again made huge efforts in June 2016 to obtain Western assistance to reach an NSG membership judgement. Again, China thwarted India's efforts along with some other nations. India's biggest obstacle was its unwillingness to sign the NPT, which is the root of the

NSG regime. The India-Pakistan conflict was later another bottleneck for India during the plenary session of the NSG. [78] In support of Pakistan's reservations on India joining the party, China's opposition to India's NSG membership was read.China, which emphasised regional peace to advance economic objectives, was troubled by India's nuclear aspirations. Five underground nuclear experiments were carried out in Rajisthan on 11 May 1998. The position of India was preceded by Pakistan in Balochistan on 28May1998 by six subterranean nuclear tests. China demonstrated caution at the nuclear blasts of India but unable to purchase the grounds that India was justified. The danger from China contributed to the former conducting nuclear tests, according to India. The exposition was written in a letter to US President Bill Clinton from Indian Prime Minister Attal Bihar Vajpayee. China's assistance for Pakistan has also been stated by India as another incentive for the transfer. [79] While China was unhappy about Pakistan's nuclear testing, it laid the burden on India to launch the nuclear war in South Asia. Like China, Pakistan too has taken its nuclear tests as a 'forced answer' as the bullying mindset of India. [80] Despite the Chinese challenge. While China contested the region's nuclear arms race, it remained inclined to Pakistan.

[1] Shaolel, F. (2010)."China, US Russia trilateral relations under the context of international configuration in transition"

[2] ibid

[3] ibid

[4] Ghai, U. R. (2007). "International politics: Theory and practice".

[6] Dittmer, L. A. (1981)" The strategic triangle: An elementar game-theoretical analysis".

[7] Stange, A. S. (2015)."Synchronization in international relations: triangular interactions between China, Latin American and the United States"

[8] Smith, C. S. (2011, November 3)"the New york times"

[9] Stange, A. S. (2015). "Synchronization in international relations: triangular interactions between China, Latin American and the United States"

[10] ibid

[11] ibid

[12] ibid

[13] ibid

[14] Joseph, R. (2011)."Two eagles, one dragon: Asymmetric theory and the triangular relations between the US, China and Mexico"

[15] Ghai, U. R. (2007) " International politics: Theory and practice. Jalander"

[16] Howe, P. (1994). Paul Howe. "Review of International Studies"

[17] Thompson, K. W. (1996). "Schools of thought in international relations: interpreters, issues, and morality"

[18] Moisiu, A. (2014). "Polarity and international system consequences"

[19] Shahzad Akhtar, "Sino-Pakistani Relations: An Assessment,".

[20] Masood Khan, "Pakistan-China Business Relations".

[21] "Pak-China Trade Increases by 18.2 Percent".

[22] Mohan Guruswamy, "Pakistan-China Relations: Higher than the Mountains, Deeper than the Oceans".

[23] Abdul Qadir Memon, "Pak-China Trade: Importance of Negotiating the FTA".

[24] Noor Ahmed Memon, "Pak-China Economic and Trade Relations Remain Strong and Vibrant".

[25] Usman Shahid and Tridivesh Singh Maini, "Should Pakistan Put All Its Eggs in the China Basket?".

[26] Peer Muhammad, "Pakistan Has Failed When It Comes to Trade with China".

[27] "Preliminary Study on Pakistan and China Trade Partnership Post-FTA".

[28] Shahzad Paracha, "China and Pakistan Reluctant to Give Concessions in FTA".

[29] Khalid Mustafa, "Pakistan, China May Restart Talks on FTA-II".

[30] Paracha, "China and Pakistan Reluctant to Give Concessions in FTA II"

[31] Shahid Yusuf, "Can Chinese FDI Accelerate Pakistan's Growth?"

[32] Small, "The China-Pakistan Axis, 96"

[33] Jane Perlez, "Rebuffed by China, Pakistan May Seek I.M.F. Aid".

[34] Jafar Riaz Kataria and Anum Naveed, "Pakistan-China Social and Economic Relations".

[35] Shakeel Ahmad Ramay, "China Pakistan Economic Corridor: A Chinese Dream Being Materialized Through Pakistan".

[36] Louis Ritzinger, "The China-Pakistan Economic Corridor: Regional Dynamics and China's Geopolitical Ambitions".

[37] "Fact Book 2016: China -Pakistan Economic Corridor (CPEC)"

[38] ibid

[39] Usman Shahid, "Balochistan: The Troubled Heart of the CPEC".

[40] Mir Sherbaz Khetran, "Indian Plans to Disrupt CEPC Projects in Balochistan: Options for Pakistan"

[41] "RAW Set Up Cell to Sabotage CPEC,"

[42] Jamil Nagri, "First Trade Activity Under CPEC Kicks Off"

[43] "Today Marks Dawn of New Era': CPEC Dreams Come True" The Daily Dawn

[44] "CPEC To Add 2.5 Million New Jobs & Boost Pakistan GDP Growth to 7.5%"

[45] Abhineet Singh "Chinese Corridors And Their Economic, Political Implications For India".

[46] Danyal Hasnain Gondal, "Opinion: Turkey and Iran's Inclusion in the CPEC"

[47] Arvind Gupta and Sarita Azad, "Evaluating India's Strategic Partnerships Using Analytic Hierarchy Process".

[48] S. D. Muni and Tan Tai Yong, "A Resurgent China: South Asian Perspectives"

[49] Ayesha Siddiqa-Agha, "Pakistan's Arms Procurement and Military Buildup, 1979-99"

[50] Anwar Hussain Syed, "China & Pakistan: Diplomacy of an Entente Cordiale"

[51] Siddiqa-Agha, "Pakistan's Arms Procurement and Military Buildup"

[52] ibid

[53] ibid

[54] Syed, "China & Pakistan: Diplomacy of an Entente Cordiale"

[55] ibid

[56] Rashid Malik, "The Growing Pakistan-China Defense Cooperation".

[57] Lisa Curtis, "China's Military and Security Relationship with Pakistan".

[58] Major General Dipankar Banerjee, "Addressing Nuclear Dangers: Confidence Building Between IndiaChina-Pakistan"

[59] ibid

[60] "China Investing in Six Nuclear Projects in Pakistan" The Express Tribune.

[61] "Pakistan's Strategic Nuclear and Missile Industries."

[62] Dr Ahmad Rashid Malik, "The Growing Pakistan-China Defense Cooperation"

[63] Khan and Ahmad, "New Trends in Sino-Pak Defence and Strategic Relations since 9/11,"

[64] Jonah Blank, "Pakistan and China's Almost Alliance"

[65] Ben Quinn, "Pakistan 'Gave China Access' to Downed US Helicopter"

[66] Isaac B. Kardon, "China and Pakistan: Emerging Strains in Entente Cordiale".

[67] ibid

[68] Umbreen Javaid and Asifa Jahangir"Pakistan-China Strategic Relationship: A Glorious Journey of 55 Years"

[69] ibid

[70] " Peking Review, no. 9, 28 February 1964"

[71] "Press Conference at Dacca, 4 September 1965"

[72] "SCMP, 3336"

[73] "Dixit, op.cit, No-6, pp. 1071"

[74] "Sangat Singh, Pakistan's Foreign Policy : An Appraisal, (APH, Bombay, 1970)"

[75] "Jen - min Jih-pao, Peking Observer, 2 February 1966."

[76] Malik Ayub Sumbal, "India and the Nuclear Suppliers Group,"

[77] "Small, The China-Pakistan Axis, 51-52."

[78] Anwar Iqbal, "Formula for New NSG Members Leaves Pakistan out"

[79] Susan L. Shirk, China: "Fragile Superpower"

[80] "Lowell Dittmer, South Asia's Nuclear Security Dilemma: India, Pakistan, and China"

CHAPTER V

Areas of Concern and Implications on India

74

5.1 General

This chapter discusses ties between Pakistan and China relations and their international consequences. It based on Pakistan-China-India regional dynamism, ties with major regional players, and its effect on the relations between Pakistan and China. Two portions were included in the chapter. In the first section there is discussion of centric perspective of China and Pakistan on India. Second segment addressed how the standoff between India and Pakistan came into force over a decade and how China saw it in its neighborhood.

5.2 Pakistan's and China's India Centric Perspective

Pakistan and China have built over a period of time an India-centric outlook. The central viewpoint of Pakistan's India was to derive from the historical baggage borne by Pakistan in addition to other territorial tensions related to the ongoing conflict over Kashmir. The problem has been created by hostility, which has been affected by security constraints long after all countries' and relationships have begun. The outcome was an unsatisfactory effort by India to weaken the core interests of Pakistan. China, too, had a fractured history with India, so that Hindi Chini Bhai Bhai couldn't be short. In 1962, India and China also fought over their boundary conflict. Because of their aspirations for regional dominance and the extension of world influence, both countries pursued their competitive path, although bilaterally, in order to support each other, particularly through trade.

Pakistan and India belonged to South Asia, which is home to 1,64 billion people and accounts for 24% of the world's citizens.[1] The huge area has been interwoven with the Indian Ocean and the big mountain chains. It is dominated by the majestic mountains of the Himalayas in the north and northeast and is surrounded by the Karakorum and the Hindu Kush in the north-west. The Purvanchal Hills and Bay of Bengal are in the East while the Indian Ocean is in the South and the Arabian Sea in the South-East. In 1947, before the two states became independent of the British, the British ruled over the Indian subcontinent for almost 100 years until Pakistan and India discovered their various identities. When leaving, the British left Kashmir's unfinished agenda[2].

This could illustrate the developments of Pakistan's viewpoint on India and vice versa, with a short retrospective on events linked to Pakistan and India. After their freedom in August 1947, the ties between Pakistan and India have been stressed. Pakistan soon after independence faced huge problems, such as unequal border demarcation, widespread massacre of Muslim refugees in India, unfair divisions of military and financial properties, conflict over canal water and princely annexation of states like Kashmir, as well as numerous economic and administrative challenges. The tense ties between Pakistan and India caused and worsened most of the problems listed. The Kashmir question stayed unsolved and the safety competition between the two countries was triggered, which in 1998 became nuclear states, leading to a never-ending rally for weapons in the area. The problem was settled between the two countries. Both countries went to war four times and the situation between them was always volatile.

The 1948 Kashmir War was the first post-independence confrontation. On the eve of the partition, Maharaja Hari Singh from Kashmir was hesitant to join either Pakistan or India, as the princely countries confronted the decision to accede to one of these ruling nations. The state situation became unstable when Poonch and Mirpur's Muslim population rose up against the Maharaja. In order to promote the cause of tribal rebels passed through Kashmir on October 22, 1947 to seize Srinagar. Maharaja Hari Singh called for Indian help in the face of the tough circumstance. The support has been given, but the accession to India has been accepted by Maharaja. This resulted in war between Pakistan's armies and India. This inconclusive war ended with a cease fire on 1 January 1949, when the military of the two nations, under the terms of Karachi, placed along the control lines (LoC).

The second big confrontation between Pakistan and India on the Jammu and Cashmere problem occurred in September 1965. With an all fighting was followed by a scam and Operation Gibraltar intended to penetrate illegal troops into the Cashmere inhabited by the Indians. [3]Thousands of causes on both sides is affected by 17-day fighting. Since the Second World War there were biggest tank fights in the war. The war concluded on 23 September 1965 after the mediation of the United Nations. Then, in January 1966, with the aid of the Soviet Mediation, the Tashkent Declaration was signed. The war has attracted the planet at large, even the major, and its geopolitical ramifications and repercussions have been diverse. In 1965 Pakistan's safety outlook with regard to India was not only stiffened by the war, but Pakistan was distasted by joining Western Alliances SEATO (1954) and CENTO (1955) to make military and political assistance available in war situations.

The Kargil conflict which began in May 1999 and ended in July was a further problem in Pakistan-India security ties. Kashmiri activists and paramilitary troops who held posts on the Indian side of the LoC occupied infiltration. On the part of Pakistan, supplies essential for India's operations at Siachen were cut and Indian soldiers were forced to withdraw. [4] The political purpose of this 'inconceived mishap' was to pursue a solution to the Kashmir conflict as Nawaz Sharif later called it, while the military goal was to generate a military challenge leading to a military solution. India reacted by heavy use of military force to Pakistan's Kargil incursion. Pakistan withdrew to its original location short of an all-encompassing escalation. Kargil had a strong effect on Pakistan-India ties, though India believed that Pakistan was an unfounded and unreliably committed ally. [5]Foundation This episode contributed also to the previous lack of confidence between the two nations.

The ties between Pakistan and India were strained for a number of reasons in the post-Kargil period. On 13 December 2001, 14 people were killed, including five jihadists, during a terrorist assault on the Indian parliament. Pakistan was accused and the military forces were mobilised. It used soldiers at the frontiers. In doing so, India warned Pakistan of India's right to dismantle Pakistan's camps and sanctuaries if the militant organisations managed to obtain funding from Pakistan as India suspected them. In the areas bordering Pakistan, India has transferred almost 500,000 soldiers. The danger faced by Indian mobilisation was also pushed by Pakistan to its eastern frontier. The world's forces, including the US, expected India and Pakistan.

Not only the Indian security establishment but even the ties between India and Pakistan were fatally hit. Ten terrorism organisations in ten separate places in Mumbai have been equipped with small arms and handy explosives. Over 13 million people were shocked and astounded by the attacks in Mumbai, a commercial and cultural centre. India blamed the vicious attacks immediately on Lashkar e Taiba (LeT).[6]This occurrence was another setback to the peace efforts decided upon by both nations.

The trust loss in both countries was one of their main poisoning factors. In addition to the conflicts that were mostly caused by absolute distrust, since 1947, the two countries have been near to war on several occasions. The Kashmir controversy was obviously the central driver of the partnership. Next to the terrorist issue, which was overlapping between the two nations. India said that terrorists based in Pakistan carried out attacks in 2001 and 2008, while Pakistan accused India of deliberately aiding rebels and separatists in Balochistan and offering financial help to the Tahreek e Talibaan Pakistan terrorist organization [7]. The security element in bilateral ties between the two countries was hardened by pervasive mistrust.

Relations between Pakistan and India have been characterised by antitrust and distrust since they were formed. There has already been an aura of scepticism. And if there was a moment of harmony and quiet, it was just a short time and things quickly returned to anguish and resentment. The two nations will be always in conflict with different conflicts (1948, 1965, 1971 and 1999) and crises (1987, 1990, 2001 and 2008).

Both nations have suspected one another, each other's governments, of spreading aggression and insurgents. India has consistently argued, with its aim to become a regional hegemon, that Pakistan was just a stumbling block. [8]The culture and history of incidents that coincided with the topics of this kind led to a rivalry and bitterness between the two nations. These stories may be analysed. Regardless of what Pakistan could have achieved by building stable ties with India, the central outlook for Pakistan's India was that of seeing India as an unfriendly and threatening neighbour. It is essential at this juncture to look at the central viewpoint of China's India.

From the beginning of both nations, China's Indian central outlook has undergone change. The ties between the two countries were experienced in their brief tale by "friendship, retrogression and normalization" [9]. After being declared the People's Republic India became the first non-Communist country to enter into diplomatic ties with India. Indian Premier Nehru was delighted with the Chinese revolt and strongly backed its participation in the United Nations. Nehru was not sharing the point of the United States that communism was a danger to world peace. For China Nehru felt that the battle waged by the citizens of China and their representatives was characterised by nationalism not communication.

In October 1954, Nehru visited China and was considered a significant landmark in the development of India's and China's bilateral ties. Relationships should be based on respect and honour throughout his contact with the Chinese revolutionary leader Mao Zedong. After the tour, both countries were closer together in the mid 1950's and the intimate slogan Hindi Chini Bhai Bhai often reflected the two countries' relationship. [10]Mao and Nehru were thinking at the time about various trajectories about how they should mould their respective countries.

World. World. World. In line with the Cold War, Nehru, an advocate of non-alignment, had required India to be followed by the nation. Mao, by contrast, saw the Third World arriving in the footsteps, and China's model was perfect[11]. This mirrored the mechanism of thinking leadership in terms of their respective power extension.In the mid-1950s, India and China were a good period. In 1954, the two countries signed an arrangement, in which China's claim to Tibet was applied to and confirmed. In the prelude to the same resolution became part of the popular five principles of peaceful coexistence. The Bandung Conference was preceded by 1955, a major event for African and Asian nations. Chinese Prime Minister Zhou Enlai and Indian Prime Minister Jawaharlal Nehru spoke during the conference at Bandung in order to promote the concept of unity from African Asia with a view to bringing about global peace. [12] From 1949 to 1957 this spell of peace was preserved between India and China. At this period the two countries exchanged high-level meetings. Nehru's political persuasion was partially attributed to its preservation of stability at the northeastern frontiers for almost 10 years. [13]But it was not very long for this time of friendship and stability.

Following a short bonhomie in the first half of 1959, developments weakened India and China's political and diplomatic advances in their first decade. Chinese Prime Minister Zhou Enlai asserted 90 thousand square miles of land in Ladakh in January 1959. India claimed that, by constructing a road in Aksai Chin without knowledge from New Delhi, China had encroached on Indian territories[14]. In March-April 1959 Tibetan spiritual leader Dalai Lama fled to India after this irritable demand for India. The Indian government gave him asylum.

The Indian-China ties became a turning point when China concluded India sponsored separatist forces in the Tibet area.India and China emerged as major forces in the area in the post-World War II period. The representatives of the two states were not very well aware of the fact that there was a rivalry for leadership between the rivals and the political gains of the other state would be hindered[15]. In the domain where India and China were to work, there was a will to lead and dominate politically. Therefore, apart from the boundary conflict between the two nations, the hymn of Hindi Chini Bhai Bhai and his cordial ties were terminated by a further explanation. China's leaders formed a belief that India had started to be capitalist-oriented and softened against the Western imperialism. The mantra of nonalignment was slowly but certainly discontinued, and China's heart and mind changed[16].

On 25 August 1959, as Chinese troops reached the Longju frontier, the first bloody encounter happened between India and China. An Indian soldier killed and another injured the Indians of Assam Rifles. In this connection a heated discussion on the existence of India-China ties started in the Indian Parliament. China also proceeded to reject McMahon Line's proposal that China has never signed a deal. Another meeting was held near the Kongka Pass on 21 October 1959. The fire exchange also killed nine Indian police patrol members and killed a Chinese person. [17] Tibet's crisis contributed to a widespread war between India and China in late 1962. India was uncomfortable with China's advance to Tibet in 1959, when the primary cause for the two countries' hostilities was the granting of asylum to Dalai Lama.

The exchange of fire between China and India increased after the Tibetan crisis and the asylum problem of Dalai Lama. Given the aggressive position of China, India began a future strategy in which the positions of the Chinese Prime Minister Zhou Enlai are placed well ahead. The future strategy may be a reason for Chinese leadership apprehension. In the absence of any peace, China launched an offensive and seized Rezang La and Tawang, on 20 October 1962. The unilateral truce was announced by Premier Zhou Enlai after the capture of claimed areas by Chinese troops. Ceasefire would come into force on 21 November 1962.

From 1963 to 1975 a time of stalemate followed. Sirimavo Bandaranayke (1916-2000), a Sri Lankan Prime Minister, was appointed to broker an agreement between India and China in early 1963 and appointed by "Colombo Forces." For the resolution of the conflict, she met the Chinese government. The interpreting of the proposals on which two parties reserved their consent Zhou Enlai had submitted points. [18] In September 1965 and December 1971, China also assisted India's competitor archbishop Pakistan in its fight against India. India and China were unavailable until 1976. when K R. Narayanan became the first envoy since 1962. Atal Bihari Vajpayee, India's Foreign Minister, toured China in 1979 and met Deng Xiaoping, Chairman of the Committee on Military Affairs, very warmly.[19] This was the moment for bilateral ties between the two nations. Most of this has affected the tying-up of India and China, as well as the reasons such as Tibetan territorical rivalry, Dalai Lama's escape to India and India's award of asylum in 1962 by the conflict India-China, Pakistan's nexus emergence and Chinese assistance in the 1965 and 1971 wars.

A 15 year break and a pleasure of positivity and fellowship, embodied by Deng Xiaoping. He also spoke of solving challenges if both made compromises. [20]China's Huang Hua visited India in 1981 and launched many talks on borders. Some of the boundary agreements have resulted in an impasse, but there have been negotiations. In 1987, India and China challenged each other on the Arunachal Pradesh issue, but the display of maturity on both sides somewhat avoided a warlike scenario[21].

Indian Prime Minister Rajiv Gandhi's visit in December 1988 was considered a significant achievement and a turning point in India's and China's ties. The visit was not only a part of a series of discussions on the borders but also a series of high-level visits by leading figures from each nation. During the 1990's India and China concluded a peace treaty in 1993 and 1996 to maintain peace on the LAC and to implement the confidence-building steps along the LAC. Bilateral ties were strengthened in 1990's. This flourishing bilateralism was affected when India called China a "primary strategic enemy" to rationalise its 1998 nuclear tests. [22]However, ties between the two countries were secured by ongoing agreements on border concerns and other cooperation areas.

Premier Atal Bihari Vajpayee visited China officially in June 2003. Following his arrival, eight prominent trips were made between 2003 and 2015 to representatives from both nations. Over the same time there was also an extensive exchange of senior officials. Both countries decided on appointing Special Representatives to oversee border issues during Prime Minister Vajpayee's tour. India, in particular, officially acknowledged China's Tibet assertion and opened up Nathu La for trade. A Declaration on ties and inclusive partnership concepts has also been signed in both nations. The visit to India by Chinese President Hu Jintao was very eventful from 20 November to 23 November 2006. In India, the visiting President and Indian President Abdul Kalam engaged in the Chinese-Indian Year of Friendship festivities. Both countries decided to improve their bilateral ties and established a five-year youth exchange programme. From 8 October to 17 October 2006, China visited the first delegation of this programme.[23]. Manmohan Singh from India visited China between 13 and 15 January 2008. The tour was highlighted by a private dinner for his counterpart, organised by the Chinese Premier that led to the personal relationship between the two leaders. On the occasion of the tour, the two countries signed "Shared Vision for the 21st Century." [24] The visit decided to raise bilateral trade from 40 billion to 60 billion dollars by 2010. During the visit, it was accepted.

The Indian-China ties were marked by a war and other boundary tensions and military conflicts in 1959-1962. The ties started taking a good diplomats and the economy with a 2003 visit by Prime Minister Atal Bihari Vajpayee and the exchange of visits by a range of very high level officials. A breakthrough and momentum were accelerated in the links between the two countries. [25] From 17 to 19 September 2014 Chinese President Xi Jinping visited India. A large corporate team accompanying the President of China

It aims to clarify the processes of bonhomy, war, stalemate and reconciliation in this brief account of India-China ties. Both the states that appeared in fast succession on the regional and global scenes in 1947 and 1949 also had to adapt their policies in the post-WW2 and Cold War period to the myths and realities of the bilateral, regional and foreign dictates. With the emergence of huge forces, India and China had to face two important problems, in the hope that they would lead to the remaining issues. Firstly, territorial conflicts awaited resolution on bilateral basis, and it was difficult for both countries to adjust their positions on maps and mechanisms. Secondly, it came to the question that each nation wanted to claim a greater part of regional power. Besides the conflict over boundary dispute settlement, there was also tension between two countries over the extension of regional and global control.

As the Pakistan–China view of India is discussed, it can be said that over a span of time, Pakistan and India increased conflict and rehused all the other engagements to resolve a number of problems, including the Kashmir dispute. A plot that affects the state and/or non-state players and a vast population on both sides of the frontier will be the most common narration. The bilateral perspective will probably be hostility and disagreement. For the relations between India and China; it was possible that, until a settlement to the two sides had been found, the boundary conflict would threaten to eradicate all nations.

Address political will and ability to the problem to avoid unintended effects of such confrontations. But the chances were that China's goal will continue to create discomfort in India at the strategic level with respect to South Asia and well beyond this area. And both Pakistan and China will share a focused view of India. Pakistan's approach to India was aggressive and that could be restored with the Kashmir conflict resolved. The relationship between China and India, too, will stay prudent, swinging from rivalry to competitiveness.

In this article it should be added that there was still a future without the Pakistan, China and India triangle, and this triangle looked at the difficulties, the complexity and the promises of this triangular relationship with optimism and concerns. The most affected countries are closer to these three Asian countries, and Iran and Afghanistan are nearest to each other. This will include an in-depth analysis of the ties between Pakistan, China, India, Iran and Afghanistan.

5.3 Pakistan-China Relations: Regional Impacts

This segment explains the impact on regional political, geopolitical and economic structures of Pakistan-China bilateral ties. The regional outlook has been changed as a result of events like the end of the Cold War after Soviet Union's disintegration, the advent of unipolarity, GWOT and increasing US involvement in the area, the growth of India and China, the influence of bilateral and multilateral ties among countries, and the wave of globalisation. In view of these trends, the diplomatic, strategic and economic realms of relationship between Pakistan and China continue to evolve.

Before discussing the regional and global position of China, it will still be useful to return to the debate about China as a regional and global force to count against. It had to recognise how its ties with any country might become critical and successful in this connection. Chinese researchers are split about whether China was a global force or regional power. Some scientists have argued that China is a global force now, while others will see it as a regional power. Some trends with respect to China have made the debate more intense. When China produced a miracle of prosperity, it came to the status of world power. China has now advanced from the 'periphery of the world to the middle' according to some academics and began to establish itself as a global force. Chinese academics generally considered China as a developed world and as a developing country with distinct socioeconomic metrics the international community classified this as a developing country.[26] However, China's economy has increased significantly since the early 1980's, spreading like wild fire to its status as a global force.

Indeed, the Chinese economy has a remarkable galvanising history. After 1978, China started to seek many goals in Southern Asia, following a policy of sustainable economic developments. China's objective: (1) to ensure regional peace through diplomatic means; (2) to avoid the conflicts that are not of key importance for territorial conflict and to create neutrality in territorial disputes in the region; (3) to initiate multidimensional regional cooperation; (4) to ensure continued energy supply which has become the lifeblood of the flourishing Chinese economy; (5) to support the war on terror Fifty-four Pakistan had to get prominently involved in China's regional scheme in order to achieve these goals. This overshadowed the ties of China with any South Asian nation.

China and India were obviously competing in the field with regard to regional contiguity. China has improved on its flourishing economy and reached the world in the race that seeks to expand political as well as economic strength. India responded to China's assault by modernising and strengthening its ties with the countries of Southeast and Central Asia. With the politics of multilateralism in South Asia, China prevented antagonism and encouraged regional growth. Chinese ability to rule the country has increased in both estimates, and the US as a global actor and India as a regional actor has resisted that. Fifty-fourth Multilateralism became more relevant in China's regional and global policy outlook. As far as the geopolitical periphery is concerned, China will like to exercise its power in South Asia[27].

In the regional sense, India and China have tried to strike a compromise between conflicts resulting from unresolved differences and the partnership created by both countries' ability to share economic benefits. Indian and Chinese positions have been unstable, with the neighbouring countries maintaining links and forging cooperation, which remained important in this area and had an effect on them. [28] When the Gwadar Port of Pakistan was upgraded and operationalised, China initiated a crucial move. Gwadar has had the ability to support China understand its 'Look Western' agenda and help Pakistan get a 'Look East,' a centre of strategic economic activities. Fifty-six India and China would play a major role in achieving and maintaining a regional political and economic ascendancy, which is crucial to asserting global influence.

There was a different outlook on Pakistan-China regional imperatives. Since Pakistan, China, India and the US were the main players, their interlinked pertinence fluctuated in the political as well as the strategic environment between compliments and conflictual interests in South Asia. The presence and the strength of these countries to promote their international aims rendered the policy and strategic framework work relatively complicated. In Pakistan, the US's relationships with China did not remain so warm as they were, since its partner was in battle with terror. Regardless of diplomatic attempts to enhance India-China ties, there are continuing rivalry and competitiveness between the two countries with political gaps on many questions. In the same way, China and the US continued to encounter major political and geopolitical gaps in how international and world problems were addressed, amid advancing exchange and economic relations.[29] These opposing and complementary structures influenced regional politics and had ramifications for Pakistan-China ties.

Pakistan has emerged as China's closest partner in the South Asian political milieu, and this relationship is consistent with China's aspirations and ambitions in the area. China's priority interests are balancing India, combating insurgency, and expanding economic activities in the country and beyond, and Pakistan has become a gateway for China to achieve these goals. In the regional sense, China's deep ties with Pakistan were crucial to China's security policy process, which addressed numerous concerns about India and Afghanistan. At the philosophical stage, a discussion had erupted and revolved around the notion that a balanced regional solution could be an acceptable initiative in the area, recognising India's economic ability over the conventional tilt towards Pakistan.[30] Aside from security relations with Pakistan, China will use political and economic means to achieve its regional objectives.

Pakistan, China, and India have emerged as notable representatives of a geopolitical triangle established after 1962. There were two propositions that were thought to have an effect on the three countries' interstate ties. For starters, the strategic triangle created an internal framework of "conflict development and management," albeit with little prospect of peaceful dispute resolution. Second, there were concerns of Islamic extremism and extremism that could have a detrimental impact on Pakistan-China ties. If these problems continued, one of the triangle's pillars will be diminished. If the current standoff between India and China continues, it will take on a more bilateral flavour.[31] If these propositions were tested in their historical sense, they might carry significant weight; nevertheless, regional and global changes in the last decade indicated that such a statement could not be tenable.

After all, the Indian element in Pakistan-China ties was a major concern. Real, India held a critical role in the regional triangle, and there were factors that drove India-China relations, which China often seemed to regard as essential for the regional outlook. For starters, India was a significant periphery nation that could assist China in achieving its goals of restructuring, reunification, and world peace while still pursuing shared development goals. Second, China would like to pull India into its orbit in order to dismantle the US containment policy. Third, in order to benefit from strategic, trade, and resource advantages, China would like to maintain friendly ties with South and Southeast Asian countries. Fourth, China would like to preserve good ties with the Indian Ocean force, as 50% of its oil and 80% of its overall imports move via India's coast through the Malacca Strait[32].

Various scholars' perceptions that Pakistan needed China more than China needed Pakistan, as indicated by Rizwan Zeb, were likely to shift. Outside of the CPEC agreements, which have been defined as unparalleled cooperation, four factors would have a significant impact on Pakistan-China ties. First, China spread concerns in its western province of Xinjiang, and it remained deeply worried. Second, the protection and welfare of Chinese employees employed on numerous projects within Pakistan was a major concern, as Chinese staff had already been harassed in Pakistan and continued to face threats. Third, Pakistan-China ties seemed to be government-to-government, with no people-to-people touch. This is not a good sign for potential ties. Fourth, and most notably, India will continue to project China as a challenge and develop weapons to complicate regional peace in South Asia. The issue will be exacerbated by the expansion of US-Indian military, commercial, and diplomatic relations.[33] This element will drive Pakistan and China closer together because they both trust each other.

In the triangular ties between Pakistan, China, and India, all three countries have remained occupied in a dispute framework over three questions. Kashmir is a territorial dispute between India, Pakistan, and, to a lesser extent, China. Despite causing wars between India and Pakistan, the problem remained unresolved. All nations were once on the brink of a nuclear war. Both India and China have territorial claims over Aksai Chin and Arunachal Pradesh, and both countries have gone to battle over territorial disputes, which has dampened the sense of cordiality in their ties. It should be remembered that Xinjiang, China's westernmost region, borders eight nations, including India, Pakistan, and Afghanistan. Separatists and militants in Xinjiang raised problems for China in the past, as they might find safe havens in Afghanistan and Pakistan's tribal regions.

These problems have created discord between the three countries, as each has chosen political and material assistance based on its own goals and priorities.

One might argue that the Kashmir conflict between India and Pakistan has shaped South Asia's political and strategic environment. China has always been explicit about its stance on resolving the Kashmir conflict. Its recommendation was to avert an India-Pakistan war over Kashmir because China wanted Pakistan to continue acting as a balancer to India and worried that an all-out war would destroy the illusion by decisively subjugating Pakistan. In the case of conflict, China is more likely to help Pakistan, which will be detrimental to India-China ties. China also wished to strengthen ties with South Asian countries, and the war between India and Pakistan will jeopardise this goal. Furthermore, China's support for Pakistan in its war with India will have an effect on its good and cooperative relations with other South Asian countries.[34] In terms of resolving the conflict, India would recommend that the Hunza-Gilgit region be moved to India so that China does not share a boundary with Pakistan. However, China would like to prevent the boundary between Pakistan and China from disappearing. Furthermore, as Garver argued, China could lose the power it has as a result of this conflict and may not be an ardent supporter of a Kashmir resolution.[35] Regarding China's role on Kashmir, Dr. Ahmed Rashid Malik, Director of the China Pakistan Study Centre in Islamabad, believed it would completely support Pakistan's position on the problem.

[36]In the given circumstances, there was less chance of South Asia emerging as a constructive regional integration arrangement. Disputes arose not only within regional representatives, but also within the territories of regional states. The disputes that South Asian states have been fighting for a long time will continue to exist since no successful method for resolving the issues has been devised. All diplomatic attempts made by the states involved in the conflicts showed their desire and determination to stick to their stated positions on the issues. As a result, the country would remain conflict-prone. It was a significant fact that China had emerged as a significant regional force, and regional states and the US had to adapt to this truth.

According to David Shambaugh, China's growth is one of the "principal catalysts" in forming the regional order. [37] However, there was no such paradigm that could justify the complexities of the field, and Asian scholarship usually used a variety of methods to understand how the Asian region evolved. Neither realism nor liberal institutionalism, he believes, may explain such a complex setting. As a result, China will have to determine and plan the contours of a new regional order through which China might wield political and economic power.

It should be noted here that the international imperative of Pakistan-China ties is related to the two countries' diplomatic, military, and economic standing. China has emerged as a regional force with ambitions to become a global power. Through promoting economic relations and forging trading relations with neighbouring countries, it began to expand its political and economic strength in the area. China has maintained the usage of soft power and maintained a benevolent reputation throughout its foreign ties. Despite pending border conflicts with India and other countries in its south and east, it has maintained trade and economic relations with these countries. After the realisation of its groundbreaking Belt and Road Initiative, China's outreach was likely to spread through continents, and regional countries were enticed to bind to China's mega initiative because those projects were too appealing to be overlooked or dismissed.

While becoming a nuclear force, Pakistan has been going through a tumultuous period in its history owing to insurgency, political insecurity, a lack of government, and economic difficulties. It had tense ties with India owing to border differences, as well as with an unfriendly Afghanistan in the West and an adversarial Iran. Clearly, it lacked a relaxing regional atmosphere. In this case, Pakistan-China ties with significant diplomatic, military, and economic benefits will be an excellent opportunity to investigate. An all-encompassing relationship with China will put Pakistan in a good spot, given the leverage provided by CPEC and Gwadar Port.

[1] David E. Bloom, Larry Rosenberg, and others "The Future of South Asia: Population Dynamics, Economic Prospects, and Regional Coherence"

[2] Fahmida Ashraf, "Jammu and Kashmir Dispute: Examining Various Proposals for Its Resolution"

[3] V. Ganapathy, "Military Lessons of the 1965 Indo-Pakistan War".

[4] Shahid Aziz, "Putting Our Children in Line of Fire"

[5] Peter René Lavoy, Asymmetric Warfare in South Asia:"The Causes and Consequences of the Kargil Conflict"

[6] Michael J. Fagel "Crisis Management and Emergency Planning: Preparing for Today's Challenges"

[7] Philipp Kauppert and Sarah Hees "Future Scenarios of Pakistan-India Relations".

[8] C. Christine Fair, "Fighting to the End: The Pakistan Army's Way of War"

[9] Sheikh Mohd Arif "A History of Sino-Indian Relations: From Conflict to Cooperation"

[10] Sergey Radchenko, "The Rise and Fall of Hindi Chini Bhai Bhai,"

[11] Ibid

[12] Zhang Li, "China–India Relations, Strategic Engagement and Challenges"

[13] Arif, "A History of Sino-Indian Relations"

[14] Alfred D. Low, The Sino-Soviet Dispute: An Analysis of the Polemics"

[15] Manojkumar Laxman Sali, "India-China Border Dispute: A Case Study of the Eastern Sector"

[16] ibid

[17] "Alam, Pakistan Army, Modernization, Arms Procurement and Capacity Buiding"

[18] Keshav Mishra, Rapprochement Across the Himalayas: "Emerging India-China Relations Post Cold War Period (1947-2003)"

[19] "Peter Wilson Prabhakar, Wars, Proxy-Wars and Terrorism: Post Independent India"

[20] "Maharajakrishna Rasgotra and others, The New Asian Power Dynamic"

[21] Ibid.

[22] Daniel Cheong, "Rapprochement and the Sino-Indian War of 1962"

[23] "Muthucumaraswamy Sornarajah and Jiangyu Wang, China, India and the International Economic Order"

[24] Arif, "A History of Sino-Indian Relations."

[25] Pervaiz Ali Mahesar, Ali Khan Ghumro, and Ghulam Mujtaba Khuskh, "Pakistan-China Relations: Thinking through an Indian Lens"

[26] Zhu Liqun, "China's Foreign Policy Debates"

[27] Vasiliki Papatheologou, Razwan Naseer, and Musarat Amin, "China's Engagement with Regionalization in South and Southeast Asia: A Comparative Perspective".

[28] Xiangming Chen et al., "China and South Asia: Contention and Cooperation Between Giant Neighbours,"

[29] Rajshree Jetly, "Sino-Pakistan Strategic Entente: Implications for Regional Security"

[30] Andrew Small, "Regional Dynamics and Strategic Concerns in South Asia: China's Role"

[31] "Ashok Kapur, India and the South Asian Strategic Triangle"

[32] Zeb, "Pakistan-China Relations"

[33] ibid

[34] John Garver, "China's Kashmir Policies,"

[35] ibid

[36] "Dr Ahmed Rashid Malik, The Pakistan-China Bilateral Trade"

[37] Shambaugh, "China Engages Asia"

CHAPTER VI

Conclusion

China is still affecting the South Asian safety climate in addition to the Super Powers. It is located throughout the northern border of the Indian subcontinent. The boundary between China and four of the seven South Asian countries is South Asian. In the immediate vicinity of China, Bangladesh is isolated from China by an area covering 80 km of Indian land. China is also deeply and steadfastly interested in developments in the South Asian field. In Chinese strategic thought, South Asia, as mentioned previously, takes a very important role. China has stability, status, and international and global interests in the area. China has strong links with all other South Asian countries except India, but no one is strengthened by Sino-Pak links. However, the lesser countries of South Asia have always accepted the involvement of China in South Asia because it improved its own freedom to exercise, reduced dependency on India, and eroded the preferential role played by India as a hegemon in the South Asian regional subsystem. They often benefitted from Chinese help and military supplies and rhetorical or even diplomatic support if sometimes needed.

China is not super strength & is between super power and medium power. China is not super power. But most China's helps are ideologically driven like the Super Powers and their military and economic assistance is no exception, either. For economic benefits like France or Great Britain, China provides military and financial aid to its friends and partners, albeit in search of geopolitical policies. But China's Military and Economic Assistance programmes have been bound from the very beginning by the limits of its fragile economic and development capability constraints. The number of Chinese armed countries and the number of economic aid countries has substantially increased since 1964. In addition, China's quality and range of arms has increased. "China's military assistance catalogue does not have a very limited variety of offerings from the Super Powers. China has sold everything to jet aircraft and warships, from granadas and rifles." [1] The Chinese help kit does, however, have certain distinctive features. First of all, for a number of purposes, state and movements benefiting from Chinese assistance were chosen. An study of support trends shows how Beijing policy preferences are shifting. China began its Military Assistance

Policy by sending weapons for what it thought of as the war against colonial and Colonial domination to its neighbours, such as Vietnam and Kampuchea. China started arming Pakistan as a countervailing power for India by worsening Chinese-Soviet and China-Leninian links in the late fifties and early sixties. Again, China has begun to provide South Asian countries around India military support, as a strategy of containment, with the steady rise in India's strength and dominance in the South Asian region and its increased Soviet involvement. Finally, shipments of Chinese weapons to countries in the Middle East for gains have increased. Late in the year even, weapons sales to numerous Southern Asian countries were gradually, but slowly declining, like Pakistan, as Chinese-Soviet and Chinese-Lndian ties were normalised! Second, Chinese firearms are far more reliable with their accuracy than those of the Soviets or the western countries. This was partly attributed to the Chinese economy's relative backwardness. The earlier Chinese arms, however, were mostly variants from the Soviet 1950s model and hence were often obsolete and laggered behind Western and Soviet goods. But that does not imply the usefulness of the Chinese firearms. In contrast, Chinese firearms is more appropriate in the rough environments of the Third World where the most modern, advanced technology is not always required. The Chinese also used further to resolve the disadvantage in the efficiency and relative lack of advanced firearms. Chinese assistance's third component is transfers, which were a distinguishing feature of the Chinese programme. Both military and economic assistance from China was free before the eighties - including direct grants or free interest loans. SIPRI states however that there is nothing understood regarding Chinese credit terms and ways of payment and that the Chinese argument that the PRC is the only nation free from arms cannot be justified. In the past, the Chinese allegedly declined to pay the arms by saying: "We're not arms dealers." The President of Egypt Mubarak spoke about the very fair rates in China, although in Pakistan recorded paying just half the price to aircraft bought from China that similar aircraft in Western countries would have charged. But China was still unable to sell sophisticated and specialised military vehicles, which might raise costs by the end of the 1970s. The States that had been as expensive as the West without matching their complexity may not have been involved in the use of Chinese firearms either. Thus, "By having better conditions, China tried to compensate for its low weapons. Essentially, China had no alternative, or its military support might not be enticing." [2] But in the

1980s, China became a profitable source of hard currency revenues for military assistance. A Chinese military officer summarise the modified Chinese weapons market philosophy: "We can't always sell at friendship rates." [3] For China's own modernization and to finance its own R&D programme, foreign currency was essential. The military assistance programme of China is revolutionary and beneficial to the receiving exchange officer. It is more adapted to the requirements and relatively sophisticated and generous conditions of beneficiaries, and military assistance in China causes minimal dependency." [4] Fourthly, China supplied only small arms in the original years, as the PLA was not suddenly needed and Chinese economy was less strained. In addition, small arms were simpler to carry and China had logistical challenges of a long scale. However, in the mid-sixties, some main allies such as Pakistan were provided with heavy weapons. [5]But in the '70s, China started to export more heavy naval weapons, mostly to Pakistan including submarines and destroyers. But China started licencingcoproductions instead of losing its own account, as special quality steel was scarce. [6] This was part of China's increasing drive to licence co-production in the 1970s. China's rejection of transferring technologies has not led China to join the ranks of major weapons provider countries that have awarded approved manufacturers to customer States. The reach of Chinese assistance in this sector was small, as most Chinese aid beneficiaries were underdeveloped countries with no major arms production facilities. And the countries with facilities refused to co-produce the obsolete machinery of China. Fifthly, economic assistance has an advantage over military aid in the overall Chinese policy. But this too was evolving by the late 1980s, as did Chinese foreign policy. Without granting them military assistance, e.g. Nepal, China had once extended economic help to nations, but never did the contrary. Pakistan was the sole exception receiving more military support than economic assistance.

World political countries' bilateral or multilateral ties have been analysed from both a realistic viewpoint and an interdependence perspective. Ties between Pakistan and China were studied through two contending paradigms, namely realism and dynamic interdependence, in terms of international relations theories. The explanation of the interconnection from the hypothetical world of philosophy to the actual field of policy of both states was alluded to as a variety of assumptions. Pakistan and China have been more and more interdependent over time, in the form of all-encompassing economic collaboration including oil, infrastructure and trade. This collaboration and interdependence was demonstrated by links formed in various channels, including the government and private sectors, the NGO elite, banks and business organisations, between the two countries over the last five decades. The paradigms of dynamic interdependence were relatively important and better characterised the relationship between Pakistan and China in this sense, a bilateral Pakistan-China relationship.

Realistically speaking, strategic stability had overshadowed many of the State goals and the environment as a whole will appear to be slave to the security factor dictated by force of foreign relations. From a realistic point of view, countries will launch a defence race to gain influence to improve their stature in international affairs. Significantly, in regional and international affairs, Pakistan and China faced separate situations when each country had various security challenges. As a growing global and regional influence, China has been confronted with security issues in East Asia and South Asia as a consequence of international security rivalry to restrict China's expansionary nature. The unresolved territorial conflicts often meant that Paquistan had defence imperatives with respect to India. Theory then dealt with bilateral relations through theoretical elements of dynamic interdependence while realism, given their safety issues in the respective security realms, clarified 'Pakistan-China links' though not aimed at one another. In Pakistan-China ties, the result of interdependence had become economic necessity, and realism was the result of political necessity.

Diplomatic ties between Pakistan and China started in 1949 and continued through numerous changes at the international, local and national levels. Three separate stages of historical development occurred in ties between the two nations. The first step was about the Cold War in which, due to its intellectual foundations, Pakistan-Chana ties were originally characterised with rejection and hesitation, but later moved towards unity and cordiality. Pakistan and China established profound cooperation in the second period that started after the Cold War. It was a time when China emerged as a major economic driver, and after the Soviet Union's disintegration the world strained to accommodate the US primacy.

The rivalry between the two world powers, in Pakistan's geographic proximity to China, was carried out during the Cold War era. Pakistan opted for a part in US-backed alliances such as SEATO and CENTO that alienate the Soviet Union, in order to address its concerns about security. China also had reservations about Pakistan's alliance and foreign policy initiatives choices. In the period when States joined either of the two power centres that had global reach and influence, India decided to remain unallocated. During this period, India also came near China. In the Cold War policy, China decided to rely on the Soviet Union, while the US sought State support to fight the Communist Soviet Union's expansionist plans.

Not only globally and regionally, but domestic and behavioral incidents and issues affected Pakistan and China. In Pakistan during the Indian-Pakistan War of 1965, the war of 1971, and the disintegration of Pakistan, Pakistan was deeply influenced by the Soviet invasion of Afghanistan and Pakistan's status as soldier. Similarly, events that shaped the situation of China were the Soviet invasion by Afghanistan and Tiananmen Square. In addition, the 1949 revolution and the CPC took control, a huge leap forwards, cultural revolutions, and the 1978 reforms and openings.

There was a shift towards the end of the Cold War in regional and world political alignments. After the global disintegration of the Soviet Union, the US started to use its leverage as the only superpower. Meanwhile, China has started to expand its regional and global influence with its economic reforms and the opening of its agenda. After the Soviet disintegration, India began to re-orient and redirect itself to the US, projected to be the largest market and democracy. Pakistan, that worked in the Soviet invasion of Afghanistan and engaged with the US for nearly a decade, faced US displeasure with a desire to acquire nuclear weapons. With Pakistan and China becoming rational political, strategic and economic allies in this situation, when the US began distancing itself from Pakistan.

China was concerned about the US involvement in its immediate neighborhood, and Pakistan became an important ally in the US campaign. Somehow, Pakistan might assure China that their alliance with the US would be in some way a compulsion, that Pakistan's closeness with the US would not affect Pakistan-China relations under these circumstances and had nothing to do with China. However, for India, Pakistan-US cordiality was not welcome or could reduce India's regional hegemonic ambition.

During its wars with India, China had supported Pakistan. Following the country's 1971 debacle, China provided every support and helped Pakistan to become military self-sufficient in order to thwart any further possibility. China has assisted Pakistan in achieving its nuclear energy acquisition objectives by achieving material, expertise and technology. The need for China to neutralize the effect of Indian aspiration of expanding its influence was driven by China's strategic support for Pakistan and consequent military cooperation.

Pakistan and China signed a comprehensive nuclear agreement in 1986 and during their visit to Pakistan, in 1989, Mr Li-Peng and Mr Jiang Zemin signed the comprehensive nuclear agreement in 1996. China has not only provided Pakistan with military hardware since 1964, but has also helped build different Pakistani factories to indigenize its defence facilities.

Economic relations between Pakistan and China included trade, investment, energy and the development of infrastructures. The CPEC, which is known as a game changer, would bring the economic relations between both countries to a higher point as huge investments of $50 billion would flow and much more would follow. The major advantage, in addition to connectivities from China's Xinjiang province to Pakistan's Gwadar port, is the energy projects planned to build in different areas in Pakistan that Pakistan will gain from this relationship. With this investment, Pakistan's economic outlook would change.

China would aspire to become both a regional and global power in terms of its political, strategic and economic stature over a period. With successful economic reforms at home forging strategic and economic co-operation with peripheral countries, China began exhibiting its political and economic influence in this whole region. In its diplomatic ties, China preferred soft power to represent its benevolent portrait. While it still had unresolved border conflicts with India and its southern and eastern countries, it also had trade and economic relations with them briefly. When its groundbreaking Belt and Road Initiative was implemented, China's approach connected the continents. Regional countries would like to link up with China's mega-initiatives in their interests. This will put China in the region's higher pedestal.

While Pakistan is a nuclear force, insurgency, political instability, a lack of direction, and economic problems have taken a tough time in its history. Due to stressful ties with India due to border conflicts, unfavorable Afghanistan and aggressive Iran, Pakistan did not enjoy a secure location in regional settings. In this scenario Pakistan and China will be an excellent opportunity to examine the ties with major diplomatic, geopolitical and economic gains. All-embrace ties with China will place Pakistan in a position to deal well with oil, trading and infrastructure problems, in particular by using the leverage of CPEC and Gwadar Port. Comprehensive collaboration between Pakistan and China may theoretically tackle multiple challenges in Pakistan, allowing Pakistan to make a contribution in asserting its place in regional political circles.

After the end of the Cold War, Chinese ties with India have strengthened. Though both countries fought against borders in 1962 and exposed the strategic weakness of India to China in the first place, the repercussions of the war could never undermine the common ties in commerce and the economy of both countries. Despite concerns from China concerning border tensions with India, trade between the two countries has gradually increased, from $52.14 billion in 2016 to $65 billion by 2017. Bilateral trade between the two countries is projected to grow. About the reality that China would never allow India to extend its political influence beyond what might thwart Chinese regional ambitions, China will continue to wave its territorial conflicts with India and concentrate on trade and economic development.

China wished to build close ties with the Middle East not only to satisfy its energy requirements, more than half of which were supplied by Middle East countries, but also to avoid sectarian and religious rivalry across Saudi-Iran and Iran-Israel confrontationist relations from being dominated by the Belt & Road Initiative. China played a crucial role in the conclusion, by withdrawing Iran from the negative impact of decades-old sanctions, of the nuclear deal between Iran and the P5+1 powers. In the growth of Iran's nuclear and missile programs, China made major investments. China has recently spent billions of dollars in Iran's energy industry in order to maintain a constant supply of Iranian oil into the Chinese market, after economic ties that have become the focus of China's foreign politics against Iran. In its area of power, China would like to see Iran, politically and economically prosperous.

Over the decades, ties between China and Pakistan have grown from neighbors to all-weather allies, built on shared confidence and cooperation. Pakistan in the region has supported China's position on issues of its national interest, such as the One China policy and vice versa. In the development of conventional defense ammunition plants, China sponsored Pakistan, as well as the rocket and nuclear programmes. Economically, CPEC added a new dimension to bilateral ties by providing China with an alternative path to the outside world for communication and providing Pakistan with a rare chance to improve its economic growth. China will like to see a secure and economically peaceful Pakistan bordering its western province of Xinjiang, and China will continue to assist Pakistan in this endeavour. China will also expect Pakistan to check India and oppose any increase in India's regional presence that could jeopardise China's interests in the area.

Pakistan-India ties have been hampered by flawed diplomacy. Both countries did not believe it was enough to put their thorny problems on hold for the time being in order to offer peace a reasonable chance. Since their emergence, both countries have been in a confrontational mode, which not only dominated their governments, but also generated an aggressive public mood climate. The effect is a more hostile and acrimonious partnership. The unsolved Kashmir problem was the most challenging bilateral problem that had left both countries in limbo. Despite UN resolutions calling for a plebiscite into the valley, India had been determined to resolve the Kashmir question. Contrary to China, India and Pakistan could not avoid intervening with wider economic affairs. political questions. China shared Pakistan's view on India, and a reconciliation between India and Pakistan would only be feasible if both countries modified their position on the Kashmir issue.

China's regional conduct was determined and benevolent and pursued control and authority by failing to adopt a confrontational strategy, as do so usually growing power. In order to shape economic partnerships and share prosperity, China will pursue reconciliation and peace with countries at its periphery. While China had discrepancies with many countries in East Asia and South Asia, China never stopped international collaboration from being launched. As a consequence of insurgency, political unrest, development problems and the economic slowdown, and the poor ties with neighbors including Afghanistan, Iran and India, Pakistan faced a precarious situation. The good partnership of Pakistan with China in this scenario would be beneficial. Pakistan may profit from China's political and economic clout in the area to strengthen relations with neighboring countries. Positive cooperation with these countries will pay dividends in the form of regional security, stability, and development.

The global ramifications of Pakistan-China ties seemed to centre on three developments: the new world system, the India-US nuclear pact, and the United States' policy to contain China. With the signing of the Westphalian Peace in 1648 the international order became multi-polar. It represented the beginning of the national autonomy and coexistence of independent states and lasted until the end of World War II. Bipolarity was a world governance in the post-war period when America and the Soviet

Union were dragged into the tensions of the Cold War.

In the emerging order, China emerged into a solid reality for the US, with its ideology and value systems pole apart from that of the USA, would be less comfortable with competitors like China. China would have been an important player in the multi-polar world. Its political and economic expansion was significantly stimulated by his reforms and opening of 1978. In the period 2035 to 2050 China became the second biggest economy after the USA. China would exceed the US anytime according to some estimates. Although China could not achieve superpower status, only a rapid economic boost was provided, China would by all means be able to lead the fast-growing multipolar world. The U.S. too remains a key global member and maintains a strong position in world decision making, as multi-polarity does not mean a total decrease in US stature. The multi-polar world would be a welcome development for Pakistan-China relations in international policy, strategic leverage, economic cooperation.

In the Chinese immediate strategic environment, the Indian-US nuclear deal was a strategic maneuver that served India's strategic interests against Pakistan and China, but also gave the US the chance to monitor the expanding influences of China. India has earned extraordinary benefits and exceptions to this agreement, demonstrating how relevant this agreement is for the United States. Support from IAEA, NSG waiving and US official endorsement is handled by the advocates of nuclear ties between India and the US. Pakistan as the neighbor of India, with its experience of aggressive conflict with India and its nuclear arms establishment, was influenced by the Indian nuclear agreement. Indian nuclear weapons India and China were able, in spite of territorial tensions, to establish cordial ties in recent times, but China's nuclear agreement with India and US contributed to Chinese misgivings about China's view of the area. The officials in the United States said that the deal was not a motion toward China and that India preferred not to be known as China's opposite. The nuclear pact, however, will help the United States contain China and weaken Pakistan's geopolitical stance on India. The agreement would, however, provide fresh prospects for Pakistan-China policy, strategic and economic ties.

In the post-Cold War era, China's exceptional development was fantastic. China became a leading Asian country after just two decades of continuous transformation and, after becoming the second largest economy, started to compete for global stature. China's upsurge was a worldwide and regional imperative creation. Recognizing the marvel of the

Chinese rise, the United States stopped its operation to prevent China from endangering the international and global ambitions of the US. However, in order to preserve its primacy, the US also had to respond to China's regional and global scope. While the United States officials rejected China's containment, the U.S. movements in East Asia, South Asia, Central Asia and the United States suggested that China should be strongly involved in these regions. That was what the United States agreed.

The United States' revalidating or changing to the Asia policy, its military participation in Eastern Asia and its reinforcement in the periphery of China with Japan, South Korea and Taiwan will have an enormous impact on China's independence in the area. America is also helped by its role in Afghanistan and the strategic nuclear agreement with India. Many academics in the U.S. argued that the Chinese strategy must depend on containment and dedication as Chinese inclusion into the regional and global economic and political environment benefits the United States rather than isolation. As an innovative Chinese enterprise, Chinese belt and road initiatives are expected to disrupt or restore balance in Asia's containment strategies and pivotal strategies as they are leading to more than 60 countries across the continent. However, China also needs to have a balance of cordiality in its immediate surroundings and beyond.

In the light of the growing domination in South Asia, China and India have emerged as competitors. Pleasant military, strategic and economic ties were established between China and Pakistan, and good relations were formed with Afghanistan and Iran.

In order to accomplish its economic and development objectives, the main objective would be to promote and maintain stability and prosperity at the periphery. The fact that China has put up its regional conflicts with India has shown that, while having territorial disputes with it, China intends to cooperate with the regional nations. This policy would mean, in addition to diplomatic disputes, that China prioritized its economic aspirations. India, for its part, established cordial ties with Afghanistan and Iran, with the relationships encompassing all three diplomatic, military, and economic aspects. India will also like to advance its trade goals with China rather than engage in a confrontational strategy. However, India's ties with Pakistan will remain hostage to animosity and acrimony over unresolved territorial conflicts, contributing to continued mistrust.

There were reasons to believe that competition between the two countries was real when claiming room for regional power, while India and China were economically responsible for the commitment they both offered to each other in terms of economy and trade opportunity. In the realistic context, China would try to engage with India until its economic interests are served and, if China threatens China's regional interests, it undeniably begins to contain India. India saw its hegemony in the area as two threats. Firstly, China has indicated India to conduct its nuclear tests in 1998 and, secondly, Pakistan, which in the same year became a nuclear-armed state and continued its challenge to the hegemonic ambitions of India in the region. If the States regard the relationship from the prism of their interests, the competitiveness of relations would remain dominant. Engagement works if States prefer to cooperate in the context of mutual cooperation and on the basis of interdependence.

Relations between Pakistan and China have proved remarkably cordial and cooperative. In all its diplomatic initiatives, China has supported Pakistan, offered strategic support through the building, and provided incomparable economic incentives for the various sectors, including trade, energy and infrastructure. China has strengthened Pakistan's diverse stakes, reflecting the centricity of China's India. The confrontation between India and Pakistan would jeopardise the safety of the whole region and no let-up can be expected right now. This rivalry would serve China's interests in a competitive fashion with India in realistic calculations, as Pakistan could be an effort to hold India back. However, for the peace that China needs in the periphery, this conflict would be counterproductive. Pakistan-China relations would become even more friendly in both the aforementioned situations.

Globally, developments have been discussed in the study that have had a deep effect on international politics in China and the relations between Pakistan and China. International order, the Indian-US nuclear deal and America's containment strategy were emerging as key developments or as a variable. Following the 1998 nuclear tests, India and Pakistan were subject to a sanctions regime. Soon after these nuclear explosions, India and the US started nuclear talks, which later hit India with a remarkable nuclear package. With India's nuclear status, India has been hard to reach the deal, but US support has helped India eliminate the obstacles. India has not been able to achieve this. In Pakistan and China, political and diplomatic circles expressed concern about the agreement. China's scholarship raised concerns regarding US plans to contain China and was seen as being aligned with this idea. Chinese scholarship Not only did the deal give India a worldwide reputation in the nuclear sphere, but it also strengthened its position as the regional competer in China. The proximate US ally in the war on terror and longstanding Indian opponent, Pakistan felt abandoned. In addition to Pakistan and China's concerns, the world was of the view that the US could discribe nuclear weapons worldwide. The nuclear agreement between India and the US further strengthened the nuclear relationship between Pakistan and China.

Two types of responses from all over the world and the US were reportedly triggered by China's rise: commitment and restraint. The countries that wish to engage positively with China would prefer to benefit from China's accumulated economic richness over a period which has not threatened China's political or strategic interests. The countries that want to contain China will, however, anticipate and formulate their policies as a threat to their political and strategic interests. US officials and scholars contended that, rather than confronting or containing China, the United States preferred that the rise of China would run counter to US interests in the region and globally. Without openly referring to containment strategies, the United States has implemented certain initiatives that suggested that the US containment strategy of China should be the focus of the US China policy, as alliances with the China periphery countries, India's nuclear deal with the United States, and the U.S. military presence around China. This also helps build a broader relationship between Pakistan and China since Pakistan has never been part of the containment ring of China in the region.

The purpose of this study was to understand the implications of relations between Pakistan and China on India, focusing on political, strategic and economic aspects. The study examines imperatives of regional factors such as the centricity of Pakistan and China's India, the emerging relationships between Pakistan-China-India-Iran and Afghanistan as well as multilateral regional imperatives, and global implications such as the emerging international order, India-US nuclear deal and China's US containment. An obvious answer would be to launch a mechanism for peace and reconciliation to ensure peace and stability in the region and to link the region for economic dividends and collective good. Similarly, it is global to avoid political and strategic confrontation and to start a process of positive involvement. Confrontation means friction and instability, while commitment means stability and peace. Regional and international stakeholders' bilateral and multilateral involvement was the way forward if the world were to be an entirely peaceful place.

The current study has nonetheless discussed important cooperation areas and concerns regarding the relationship between Pakistan and China. The relations between the two countries were obvious, and despite several regional and global events, the relationship had flourished with the potential to build up these remarkably significant relations. It can be concluded in some trust that, despite the pressure of emerging regional and global development, these ties will continue to thrive in various areas and remain solid and mutually advantageous. This is possible, since Pakistan and China understand their connections clearly and understand the importance of relations within the framework of regional and world policies, planning and implementation. With the determination of both countries to preserve their historically fraternal ties, it is expected that they will face storms, setbacks and challenges with trust and together move forward.

The current doctoral thesis attempts to address key aspects of the research project goals. However, some aspects of the dissertation could not be covered. In fact, there are areas on which the researcher would have considered in depth but at the cost of drifting away and secondly, certain areas were so important that they could be considered as a separate project. Some of the important areas of substantialy should be recommended for thorough study and future research with regard to regional and global implications of Pakistan-China relations. Another proposals can be Iran's prospects for membership of CPEC, Pakistan as an integral part of relations between India and China, a position of major CPEC powers, prospects for regional connectivity in South Asia, a conflict of interest between Pakistan-China and India, and a policy for Pakistan in relation to China's balance with the USA.

[1] Gerald Segal & Anne Gilks, "China an the Arms Trade"

[2] "Segal & Gilks, op cit. no-1, p.262."

[3] " Wall Street Journal, 4 May 1984"

[4] "Anne Gilks & Gerald Segal, China and the Arms Trade,(Croom Helm Australia Pvt. Ltd, Sydney, 1985), p.165"

[5] "SIPRI - Arms Trade Register, also Military Balance, (MSS), 1963-1969."

[6] "Segal & Gilks, op cit. no-1, p.154"

CHAPTER VII

References

Primary Sources
Documents

1. "CPEC to Add 2.5 Million New Jobs & Boost Pakistan GDP Growth to 7.5%." South Asia Investor Review, October 7, 2016.
2. "Jen - min Jih-pao, Peking Observer, 2 February 1966
3. "Pakistan's Strategic Nuclear and Missile Industries." London: Centre for Science and Security Studies, King's College, September 2016.
4. Agreement between the Government of the People's Republic of China and the Government of the Islamic Republic of Pakistan for the avoidance of double taxation and the prevention of fiscal evasion with respect to taxes on incomeNovember 15, 1989. Accessed at http://www.chinatax.gov.cn/n810341/n810770/c1153236/part/1153237.pdf
5. China, Pakistan sign joint communiqué to cement partnership 21 December 2010 accessed at http://pk.chineseembassy.org/eng/zbgx/t779966.htm
6. China-Pakistan Dosti Zindabad speech by H.E. Xi Jinping President of the People's Republic of China 20 April 2015. Accessed at http://pk.chineseembassy.org/eng/zbgx/importantdocuments/
7. China–Pakistan Free Trade Agreement- 24th November, 2006. Accessed at http://www.tdap.gov.pk/pdf/Pak-China_FTA_Agreement.pdf
8. Congratulatory messages from H.E. Xi Jinping, President of people's Republic of China to H.E. Mamnoon Hussain, President of the Islamic Republic of Pakistan on the occasion of the 78th Pakistan Day March 23rd, 2017 accessed at http://pk.chineseembassy.org/eng/zbgx/t1448456.htm
9. Dimitrakis, Panagiotis. *Failed Alliances of the Cold War: Britain's Strategy and Ambitions in Asia and the Middle East.* Bloomsbury Publishing, 2011.
10. Dr Ahmad Rashid Malik, "The Growing Pakistan-China Defense Cooperation"
    Peking Review, no. 9, 28 February 1964, p. 9.

11. Exchange of notes on provision of Anti-Narcotics Equipment- April 20, 2015 Accessed at https://tribune.com.pk/story/876286/agreements-signed-between-pakistan-andchina/

12. Fact Book 2016: China -Pakistan Economic Corridor (CPEC)." Ministry of Planning, Development and Reforms, 2016.

13. News from Xinhua News Agency : Daily Bulletin (London), 1973-81. Peking Review (Peking),1970-1989

14. OECD Economic Surveys - China - 2015." Organisation for Economic Co-operation and Development, March 2015

15. The Boundary Agreement Between China And Pakistan, 1963 March 2, 1963

Secondary Data
BOOK

1. Ghai, U. R. (2007). International politics: Theory and practice. Jalander: New Acadomic.Co.

2. Joseph, R. (2011). Two eagles, one dragon: Asymmetric theory and the triangular relations between the US, China and Mexico. Texas, US: Baylor University in Partial.

3. Brown, Chris. *Understanding international relations.* Macmillan International Higher Education, 2019.

4. Chari, Chandra. Superpower Rivalry and Conflict: The Long Shadow of the Cold War on the 21st Century. New York: Routledge, 2009

5. Zaki, M. Akram. "China of Today and Tomorrow: Dynamics of Relations with Pakistan." *Joint Conference of the PRC Independence Day, Institute of Policy Perspective, Islamabad. Source: Compiled by Authors from different secondary data.* Vol. 23. 2010.

6. Winters, Alan, and Shahid Yusuf, eds. *Dancing with giants: China, India, and the global economy.* World Bank Publications, 2007.

7. Lo, C. K. (2003). China's Policy towards territorial disputes: the case of the South China Sea Islands. Routledge.

8. Engardio, P. A. (2006). The future of outsourcing. . Business Week, 30,, 50-64.

9. Pakistan Foreign policy", Hamid A. K. Rai (Aziz Publications : Lahore, 1981)

10. Carr, Madeline. 2016. US Power and the Internet in International Relations: The Irony of the Information Age. UK: Palgrave Macmillan.

11. Buzan, Barry; Ole Wæver and Jaap de Wilde. 1998. Security: a New Framework for Analysis. US: Lynne Rienner Publishers

12. Sampson, Anthony. *The arms bazaar*. Coronet Books, 1977

13. Englert, Matthias and Anne Harrington (2014) "How Much Is Enough? The Politics of Technology and Weaponless Nuclear Deterrence". In The Global Politics of Science and Technology - Vol. 2.

14. Englert, Matthias and Anne Harrington (2014) "How Much Is Enough? The Politics of Technology and Weaponless Nuclear Deterrence". In The Global Politics of Science and Technology - Vol. 2.

15. Small, Andrew. The China-Pakistan Axis: Asia's New Geopolitics. New York: Oxford University Press, 2015.

16. Ambedkar, B. R. Pakistan or the Partition of India. 1945. Lahore: Book Traders, 1984. Arif, K. China Pakistan Relations, 1947-1980. Lahore: Vanguard Books, 1984

17. Ebrey, Patricia Buckley, and Kwang-Ching Liu. The Cambridge Illustrated History of China. Vol. 1. London: Cambridge Univ Press, 1996.

18. Leffler, Melvyn P., and David S. Painter. Origins of the Cold War: An International History. New York: Routledge, 2005.

19. Rizvi, Dr Hassan Askari. First 10 General Elections of Pakistan. Islamabad: Pildat Publications, 2013.

20. Raghavan, Srinath. 1971: A Global History of the Creation of Bangladesh. London: Harvard University Press, 2013.

21. Andrio, Drong. "The Effects of Political Changes in the Relationship between Bangladesh and Russia (USSR) in 1971-2014." ВестникРоссийскогоУниверситетаДружбыНародов. Серия: МеждународныеОтношения, no. 1 (2015).

22. Ayesha Jalal - State of Martial Rule: Origins of Pakistan's Political Economy of Defence(1990)

1. Dawei, Cao, and Yanjing Sun. China's History. Beijing: China Intercontinental Press, 2010

24. Thompson, K. W. (1996). Schools of thought in international relations: interpreters, issues, and morality. LSU Press.

25. "Preliminary Study on Pakistan and China Trade Partnership Post-FTA." Karachi: The Pakistan Business Council, 2013.

26. Kataria, Jafar Riaz, and Anum Naveed. "Pakistan-China Social and Economic Relations." South Asian Studies 29, no. 2 (2014): 395.

27. Muni, S. D., and Vivek Chadha. Asian Strategic Review 2014: US Pivot and Asian Security. New Delhi: Pentagon Press, 2014.

28. Siddiqa-Agha, Ayesha. Pakistan's Arms Procurement and Military Buildup, 1979-99: In Search of a Policy. New York: Palgrave, 2001.

29. Hussain Syed, Anwar. China & Pakistan: Diplomacy of an Entente Cordiale. Amherst: University of Massachusetts Press, 1974.

30. Siddiqa-Agha, Ayesha. Pakistan's Arms Procurement and Military Buildup, 1979-99: In Search of a Policy. New York: Palgrave, 2001.

31. Kardon, Isaac B. "China and Pakistan: Emerging Strains in Entente Cordiale." The Project 2049 Institute, 2011.

32. Singh, Sangat, Pakistan's Foreign Policy (Bombay : Asia Publishing House, 1970).

33. Small, Andrew. The China-Pakistan Axis: Asia's New Geopolitics. New York: Oxford University Press, 2015

34. Shirk, Susan L. China: Fragile Superpower. New York: Oxford University Press, 2008

35. Dittmer, Lowell. South Asia's Nuclear Security Dilemma: India, Pakistan, and China. New York: ME Sharpe, 2005.

36. Ganapathy, V. Military Lessons of the 1965 Indo-Pakistan War. New Delhi: Citeseer, 2014.

37. Lavoy, Peter René. Asymmetric Warfare in South Asia: The Causes and Consequences of the Kargil Conflict. New York: Cambridge University Press, 2009

38. Fagel, Michael J. Crisis Management and Emergency Planning: Preparing for Today's Challenges. Florida: CRC Press, 2013.

39. Birtchnell, Thomas, Satya Savitzky, and John Urry, eds. *Cargomobilities: moving materials in a global age*. Routledge, 2015.

40. Von Schnitzler, Antina. "5. Infrastructure, Apartheid Technopolitics, and Temporalities of "Transition"." *The promise of infrastructure*. Duke University Press, 2018. 133-154.

41. Von Schnitzler, Antina. "5. Infrastructure, Apartheid Technopolitics, and Temporalities of "Transition"." *The promise of infrastructure*. Duke University Press, 2018. 133-154.

42. Peters, Susanne, and Werner Zittel. "The "Tight oil revolution" and the misinterpretation of the power of technology." *The Global Politics of Science and Technology-Vol. 2*. Springer, Berlin, Heidelberg, 2014.

83-100.

43. Guzzini, Stefano, and Dietrich Jung, eds. *Contemporary security analysis and Copenhagen peace research*. Routledge, 2003.

44. Wæver, Ole. *Securitization and desecuritization*. Copenhagen: Centre for Peace and Conflict Research, 1993.

45. Searle, John, and Daniel Vanderveken. 1985. *"Foundations of illocutionarylogic"*

46. Buzan, Barry. *People, States and Fear; The National Secutity Problem in International Relation*. The University of North Carolina Press, 1983.

47. Balzacq,T.(2005) "TheThreeFacesofSecuritization:PoliticalAgency,AudienceandContext"

48. Roy, Denny. *China's foreign relations*. Macmillan International Higher Education, 1998.

49. Kauppert, Philipp, and Sarah Hees. "Future Scenarios of Pakistan-India Relations." Dubai: Friedrich-Ebert-Stiftung (FES), May 2015.

50. Fair, C. Christine. Fighting to the End: The Pakistan Army's Way of War. New York: Oxford University Press, 2014.

51. Low, Alfred D. The Sino-Soviet Dispute: An Analysis of the Polemics. New Jersey: Fairleigh Dickinson University Press, 1976

52. Alam, Dr Shah. Pakistan Army, Modernization, Arms Procurement and Capacity Buiding. New Delhi: Vij Books India Pvt Ltd, 2012.

53. Mishra, Keshav. Rapprochement Across the Himalayas: Emerging India-China Relations Post Cold War Period (1947-2003). New Delhi: Gyan Publishing House, 2004.

54. Prabhakar, Peter Wilson. Wars, Proxy-Wars and Terrorism: Post Independent India. New Delhi: Mittal Publications, 2003

55. Rasgotra, Maharajakrishna, and others. The New Asian Power Dynamic. New York: Sage Publications, 2007.

56. Sornarajah, Muthucumaraswamy, and Jiangyu Wang. China, India and the International Economic Order. Cambridge: Cambridge University Press, 2010.

57. Kapur, Ashok. India and the South Asian Strategic Triangle. New York: Routledge, 2010 Gilks, Anne and Segal, Gerald, China and the Arms

58. Trade (Sydney : Croom Helm Australia Pvt. Ltd.), 1985).

Journal Article

1. Shaolel, F. (2010). China, US Russia trilateral relations under the context of international configuration in transition. Council on Foreign Policy, 1-30.

2. Dittmer, L. A. (1981). The strategic triangle: An elementar game-theoretical analysis. Cambrige University , 33(4), 485-515.

3. Stange, A. S. (2015). Synchronization in international relations: triangular interactions between China, Latin American and the United States. Política, Globalidad y Ciudadanía, 1(1), 24-52.

4. Howe, P. (1994). Paul Howe. Review of International Studies, 277-290

5. Moisiu, A. (2014). Polarity and international system consequences. Interdisplinary Journal of Research and Development, 1(1).

6. Akhtar, Shahzad. "Sino-Pakistani Relations: an Assessment." *Strategic Studies*, vol. 29, no. 2/3, 2009, pp. 64–80. *JSTOR*, www.jstor.org/stable/48527381. Accessed 13 May 2021.

7. Guruswamy, Mohan. "Pakistan-China Relations: Higher than the Mountains, Deeper than the Oceans." CLAWS Journal, Summer, 2010, 92–107.

8. Yusuf, Shahid. "Can Chinese FDI Accelerate Pakistan's Growth?" International Growth Centre 4 (2013).

9. Small, Andrew. *The China Pakistan axis: Asia's new geopolitics*. Random House India, 2015.

10. Ramay, Shakeel Ahmad. "China Pakistan Economic Corridor: A Chinese Dream Being Materialized Through Pakistan." Sustainable Development Policy Institute, 2016.

11. Ritzinger, Louis. "The China-Pakistan Economic Corridor: Regional Dynamics and China's Geopolitical Ambitions." The National Bureau of Asian Research, August 5, 2015.

12. Khetran, Mir Sherbaz. "Indian Plans to Disrupt CEPC Projects in Balochistan: Options for Pakistan." Islamabad: Institute of Strategic Studies, September 28, 2016.

13. Singh, Abhineet. "Chinese Corridors And Their Economic, Political Implications For India." Swarajya, June 7, 2016.

14. Gupta, Arvind, and Sarita Azad. "Evaluating India's Strategic Partnerships Using Analytic Hierarchy Process." Institute for Defence and Analyses. September 17 (2011): 2011.

15. Rashid Malik, Dr Ahmad. "The Growing Pakistan-China Defense Cooperation." Islamabad: Institute of Strategic Studies, October 7, 2016.

16. Curtis, Lisa. "China's Military and Security Relationship with Pakistan," May 20, 2009.

17. Banerjee, Major General Dipankar. "Addressing Nuclear Dangers: Confidence Building Between India-China-Pakistan." India Review 9, no. 3 (2010): 345–363.

18. Khan, Zahid Ali, and Shabir Ahmad. "New Trends in Sino-Pak Defence and Strategic Relations since 9/11: Indian Concern." South Asian Studies 30, no. 2 (2015): 247

19. Blank, Jonah. "Pakistan and China's Almost Alliance." Foreign Affairs, October 15, 2015.

20. Javaid, Umbreen, and Asifa Jahangir. "Pakistan-China Strategic Relationship: A Glorious Journey of 55 Years." Journal of the Research Society of Pakistan 52, no. 1 (2015)

21. Dixit, Aabha, "Enduring Sino-Pak Relations : The Military Dimension", Strategic Analysis, vol. 12, no.9, December 1989, pp. 981-992.

22. Dixit, Aabha, "Sino-Pak Relations and their Implications for India", Strategic Analysis, vol. 11, no.9, December 1987, pp. 1067-80.

23. Bloom, David E., Larry Rosenberg, and others. "The Future of South Asia: Population Dynamics, Economic Prospects, and Regional Coherence." WDA-Forum, University of St. Gallen, 2011

24. Ashraf, Fahmida. "Jammu and Kashmir Dispute: Examining Various Proposals for Its Resolution." Islamabad Papers, ISSI 20 (2002)

25. Arif, Sheikh Mohd. "A History of Sino-Indian Relations: From Conflict to Cooperation." International Journal of Political Science and Development 1, no. 4 (2013): 129– 137.

26. Radchenko, Sergey. "The Rise and Fall of Hindi Chini Bhai Bhai." Foreign Policy, September 18, 2014.

27. Li, Zhang. "China–India Relations, Strategic Engagement and Challenges." Asie. Visions, no. 34 (2010)

28. Arif, Sheikh Mohd. "A History of Sino-Indian Relations: From Conflict to Cooperation." International Journal of Political Science and Development 1, no. 4 (2013): 129– 137.

29. Cheong, Daniel. "Rapprochement and the Sino-Indian War of 1962." Ezra's Archives, 2015.

30. Ali Mahesar, Pervaiz, Ali Khan Ghumro, and Ghulam Mujtaba Khuskh. "Pakistan-China Relations: Thinking through an Indian Lens." International Journal of Scientific Research and Innovative Technology, no. Vol. 3, No. 3 (March 2016).

31. Majie, Zhu. "China and Asia-Pacific Security Building in the New Century." Asia-Pacific Security: Policy Challenges, 2003, 61

32. Papatheologou, Vasiliki, Razwan Naseer, and Musarat Amin. "China's Engagement with Regionalization in South and Southeast Asia: A Comparative Perspective." South Asian Studies 29, no. 1 (2014): 281–290

33. Chen, Xiangming, Pallavi Banerjee, Gaurav I. Toor, and Ned Downie. "China and South Asia: Contention and Cooperation Between Giant Neighbours." The European Financial Review, May 2014.

34. Jetly, Rajshree. "Sino-Pakistan Strategic Entente: Implications for Regional Security." Institute of South Asian Studies, 2012.

35. Andrew Small, "Regional Dynamics and Strategic Concerns in South Asia: China's Role," Centre for Strategic & International Studies (CSIS), 2014, 8.

36. Zeb, Rizwan. "Pakistan-China Relations: Where They Go from Here?" UNISCI Discussion Papers, no. 29 (2012): 45.

37. Garver, John. "China's Kashmir Policies." India Review 3, no. 1 (2004): 1–24

38. Malik, Ahmad Rashid. "The Pakistan-China Bilateral Trade: The Future Trajectory." *Strategic Studies*, vol. 37, no. 1, 2017, pp. 66–89. *JSTOR*, www.jstor.org/stable/48535987. Accessed 13 May 2021.

39. Shambaugh, David. "China Engages Asia: Reshaping the Regional Order." International Security 29, no. 3 (2005)

40. Memon, Noor Ahmed. "Pak-China Economic and Trade Relations Remain Strong and Vibrant." Chinese Review(2016)

41. Chaudhry, Praveen K., and Marta Vanduzer-Snow. The United States and India: AA History Through Archives

42. Kenneth E. Boulding, "Integrative Aspects of International System", Proceedings of the International Peace Research Associations (VAN Gorcum, Assen, 1966), p.27.

43. Kumar, S. (2007). The China– Pakistan Strategic Relationship: Trade, Investment, Energy and Infrastructure. . Strategic Analysis, 31(5),, 757-790.

44. Kumar, S. (2007). The China– Pakistan Strategic Relationship: Trade, Investment, Energy and Infrastructure. . Strategic Analysis, 31(5),, 757-790.

45. Haider, Ziad. "Sino-Pakistan Relations and Xinjiang's Uighurs: Politics, Trade, and Islam along the Karakoram Highway." Asian Survey 45, no. 4

(2005): 522–545

46. Deepak, B. R. (2006). Sino-Pak 'Entente Cordiale'* and India ALook into the Past and Future. China report, 42(2), 129-151.

47. Khokhar, A. Y. (2011). Sino-Indian relations: implications for Pakistan. Institute of Strategic Studies. Islamabad.

48. Young, S. M. (2015). US–China Relations. . American Foreign Policy Interests, 37(5-6),, 264-272.

49. Malik, H. Y. (2012). Strategic Importance of Gwadar Port. . Journal of Political Studies, 19(2), 57

50. Kumar, S. (2007). The China– Pakistan Strategic Relationship: Trade, Investment, Energy and Infrastructure. . Strategic Analysis, 31(5),, 757-790.

51. Haider, Ziad. "Sino-Pakistan Relations and Xinjiang's Uighurs: Politics, Trade, and Islam along the Karakoram Highway." Asian Survey 45, no. 4 (2005): 522–545.

52. Sharma, B.L., (1969), Asia: Pakistan in Crisis By G.S. Bhargava. Vikas, Delhi. 1969. 222p. , *India Quarterly: A Journal of International Affairs*, 25, issue 3, p. 272-273

53. Hansen, Lene and Helen Nissenbaum. 2009. "Digital Disaster, Cyber Security, and the Copenhagen School". International Studies Quarterly. 53(4): 1155-1175.

54. Englert, Matthias and Anne Harrington (2014) "How Much Is Enough? The Politics of Technology and Weaponless Nuclear Deterrence". In The Global Politics of Science and Technology - Vol. 2.

55. Hecht, Gabrielle. 2010. "The Power of Nuclear Things". Technology and Culture. 51: 1-30.

56. Singh, P. (2015). The China Pakistan Economic Corridor and India. . IDSA Comment,

57. Pitlo III, L. B. (2015). China's One Belt, One Road to Where?'. . The Diplomat, 17.

58. Pehrson, C. J. (2006). String of pearls: Meeting the challenge of China's rising power across the Asian littoral. . ARMY WAR COLL STRATEGIC STUDIES INST CARLISLE BARRACKS PA

59. Kukeyeva, F. T. (2012). NEW FIVE DIMENSIONS OF GLOBAL SECURITY. .ВестникКазНУСерияМеждународныеотношения и международноеправо, 57(1).

60. Rajain, A. (2005). Nuclear Deterrence in Southern Asia: China, India and Pakistan. . SAGE Publications India

61. Small, A. (2015). The China-Pakistan Axis: Asia's New Geopolitics. . Oxford University Press. Syed, A. (1969). Sino-Pakistan Relations—An Overview. . Pakistan Horizon, 22(2),, 107-119.

62. Garver, J. W. (1996). Sino-Indian Rapproachement and the Sino-Pakistan Entente. . Political Science Quarterly, 111(2), , 323-347

63. Andrew J. Pierre – "The Global Politics of Arms Sales" (New Jersey: Princeton Univ. Press, 1982

64. Anne Gilks and Gerald Segal – "China and the Arms Trade" (Sydney: Croom Helm, 1985)

65. Michael Brozska and Thomas Ohlson – "Arms Transfers to the Third World: 1971" - 85 (SIPRI, London: OUP, 1986

66. S. M. Burke, "Pakistan's Foreign Policy: An Historical Analysis", (Oxford University Press, London, 1973)

67. Collier, Stephen J. and Andrew Lakoff. 2008. "The Vulnerability of Vital Systems: How "Critical Infrastructure" Became a Security Problem". In The Politics of Securing the Homeland: Critical Infrastructure, Risk and Securitisation. Dunn, Myriam and Kristian SobyKristensen (eds.). London: Routledge.

68. Cowen, Deborah. 2010a. "A Geography of Logistics: Market Authority and the Security of Supply Chains". Annals of the Association of American Geographers 100(3): 600-620.

69. Cavelty, Myriam Dunn. 2012. "TheMilitarisation of Cyber Security as a Source of Global Tension". In Strategic Trends Analysis. Möckli, Daniel and Andreas Wenger (eds.). Center for Security Studies. 103-124.

70. Hecht, Gabrielle. 2010. "The Power of Nuclear Things". Technology and Culture. 51: 1-30.

71. Hecht, Gabrielle. 2001. "Technology, Politics, and National Identity in France". In, Allen, Michel T. and Gabrielle Hecht (eds.). Technologies of Power. London: The MIT Press. 253-293.

72. Kurban, Can; Ismael Peña-López and Maria Haberer. 2017. "What is Technopolitics? A Conceptual Schema for Understanding Politics in the Digital Age". IDP Revista de Internet, Derecho y Política. 24: 3-20.

73. Britt; Michael Webber and Sarah Rogers. 2017. "The Techno-Politics of Big Infrastructure and the Chinese Water Machine". Water Alternatives. 10(2): 233-249.

74. Edwards, Paul N. and Gabrielle Hecht. 2010. "History and the Technopolitics of Identity: The Case of Apartheid South Africa". Journal

of Southern African Studies. 36(3): 619-639.

75. Hecht, Gabrielle. 2001. "Technology, Politics, and National Identity in France". In, Allen, Michel T. and Gabrielle Hecht (eds.). Technologies of Power. London: The MIT Press. 253-293.

76. Chacko, Priya. 2019. "Constructivism and Indian Foreign Policy". In New Directions in India's Foreign Policy: Theory and Praxis. Pant, Harsh V (Ed.). UK: Cambridge University Press. 48-66.

77. Mayer, Maximilian; Mariana Carpes and Ruth Knoblich (Eds.). Berlin: Springer-Verlag. 287-302.

78. Mayer, Maximilian; Mariana Carpes and Ruth Knoblich (Eds.). Berlin: Springer-Verlag. 205-220.

79. Collier, Stephen j. and Andrew Lakoff. 2015. "Vital Systems Security: Reflexive Biopolitics and the Government of Emergency". Theory, Culture & Society 32(2): 19–51.

80. Mann, Michael. 1984. "The Autonomous Power of the State, its Origins, Mechanisms and Results".European Journal of Sociology. 25(2): 185-213.

81. Levine, J. H. (1972). The sphere of influence. . American Sociological Review,, 14-27.

82. Jaffrelot, C. (2003). India's look east policy: an Asianist strategy in perspective. . India Review, 2(2),, 35-68.

83. Egreteau, R. (2008). India's Ambitions in Burma: More Frustration Than Success??. . Asian Survey, 48(6),, 936-957.

84. Naseer, Rizwan, and Musarat Amin. "Syed , A. (1969): A Natural Allianceagainst Common Threats." Berkeley Journal of Social Sciences 1, no. 2 (2011): 1–

85. Dobell, W. M. "Ramifications of the China-Pakistan Border Treaty." Pacific Affairs 37,no. 3 (1964): 283–295.

86. Varshney, Ashutosh. "India, Pakistan, and Kashmir: Antinomies of Nationalism." Asian Survey 31, no. 11 (1991): 997–1019.

87. Cao, Lan. "Chinese Privatization: Between Plan and Market." Law and Contemporary Problems 63, no. 4 (2000): 13–62.

88. Siddiqui, AzharJaved, and Khalid Manzoor Butt. "Afghanistan-Soviet Relations during the Cold War: A Threat for South Asian Peace." South Asian Studies 29, no. 2 (2014): 617.

89. Sternthal, Susanne. "Unraveling the Soviet Union: Gorbachev's Change in World View."Demokratizatsiya, 1998, 453–454.

90. Mukerji, Chandra. "The territorial state as a figured world of power: Strategics, logistics, and impersonal rule." *Sociological Theory* 28.4 (2010): 402-424.

91. Balzacq, Thierry. "The three faces of securitization: Political agency, audience and context." *European journal of international relations* 11.2 (2005): 171-201.

92. Vuori, Juha A. "Illocutionary logic and strands of securitization: Applying the theory of securitization to the study of non-democratic political orders." *European journal of international relations* 14.1 (2008): 65-99.

93. "Tibetan Uprising of 1959 referred to the rebellion that began in the capital of Tibet, Lhasa. A conflict that started between Tibetan rebels and Chinese army in 1956 in Kham and Amdo regions intensified in March 1959. The guerilla war continued till 1962

94. Naseer, Rizwan, and Musarat Amin. "Sino-Pakistan relations: A natural alliance against common threats." *Berkeley Journal of Social Sciences* 1.2 (2011): 1-11.

Magazine

1. Shahid, Usman, and Tridivesh Singh Maini. "Should Pakistan Put All Its Eggs in the China Basket?" The Diplomat, July 22, 2016.

2. Usman Shahid and Tridivesh Singh Maini, "Should Pakistan Put All Its Eggs in the China Basket?," The Diplomat, July 22, 2016

Website

1. Hasnain Gondal, Danyal. "Opinion: Turkey and Iran's Inclusion in the CPEC." Pakchinanews.pk, September 20, 2016. http://pakchinanews.pk/opinion-turkey-andirans-inclusion-in-the-cpec/.

2. Board of Investment accessed at: http://boi.gov.pk/InfoCenter/CPEC.aspx China Council for the Promotion of International Trade accessed at: http://english.ccpit.org/

3. China Pakistan Economic Corridor: accessed at: http://www.cpecinfo.com/ CPEC accessed at: http://cpec.gov.pk/

4. CPEC: China Pakistan Economic Corridor, January 23, 2017. http://cpec.gov.pk/special- economic-zones-projects#.

5. Gul, Ayaz. "China Delivers First Batch of Military Aid to Afghanistan."Http://Www.voanews.com, July 3, 2016.

6. Hasnain Gondal, Danyal. "Opinion: Turkey and Iran's Inclusion in the CPEC." Pakchinanews.pk, September 20, 2016. http://pakchinanews.pk/opinion-turkey-and- irans-inclusion-in-the-cpec/.

7. India - China Relations: Embassy of India, Beijing, January 2016. http://indianembassy.org.cn.

8. Korab-Karpowicz, W. Julian. "Political Realism in International Relations," 2010. http://stanford.library.usyd.edu.au/entries/realism-intl-relations/.

9. Ministry of Planning Development & Reform accessed at: http://www.pc.gov.pk/ Nihao-salam accessed at: http://www.nihao-salam.com/

10. Pakistan Business Council accessed at: http://www.pbc.org.pk/ Pakistan China Institute accessed at: http://www.pakistan-china.com/ Pakistan China Investment Company Limited: accessed at:http://www.pakchinainvestment.com/

11. Pakistan China Joint Chamber of Commerce accessed at: http://www.pcjcci.org/ The World Factbook." Central Intelligence Agency:

12. https://www.cia.gov/library/publications/the-world-factbook/geos/ch.html.

13. Trade Development Authority of Pakistan accessed at: http://www.tdap.gov.pk/pakistan- china-trade-relations.php

News paper article

1. Khan, Masood. "Pakistan-China Business Relations." Daily The Nation

2. "'Today Marks Dawn of New Era': CPEC Dreams Come True." The Daily Dawn, November 13, 2016.

3. "China Appoints Special Envoy for Afghanistan." Daily The Nation. July 19, 2014. "China Firm Aims to Build Big Nuclear Plant for Pakistan." The Express Tribune, September 20, 2010.

4. "China Investing in Six Nuclear Projects in Pakistan." The Express Tribune, February 9, 2015.

5. "China, Pakistan Highlight Cooperation in Beijing." People's Daily, November 4, 2003. "China, Pakistan Issue Joint Statement, Vow to Deepen Cooperation." Beijing Review,May 24, 2013.

6. "China: Afghanistan Backs Beijing Stance on South China Sea." The Daily Mail. May 16, 2016.

7. "Ghani Seeks Chinese Investment in First Foreign Trip." The Daily Dawn. October 28, 2014.

8. "Musharraf Wraps up State Visit to China." People's Daily, April 16, 2008. "Pak-China Trade Increases by 18.2 Per cent." The Daily Dawn. April 27, 2016. "Pakistan-China Relations." China Daily. November 14, 2006.

9. "Proclamation of the Central People's Government of the PRC." People's Daily, October 2, 1949.

10. "RAW Set Up Cell to Sabotage CPEC." The Express Tribune. April 14, 2016.

11. "Respect Pakistan Sovereignty, China Tells US." The News International. May 19, 2011. "Special Force Set Up to Guard Gwadar Port's Sea Lanes." The Daily Dawn. December12, 2016.

12. Abrar Saeed, and Maqbool Malik. "Pakistan, China Begin an Epoch Unparalleled." Daily The Nation. April 21, 2015.

13. Anwar Iqbal. "Formula for New NSG Members Leaves Pakistan out." Daily Dawn, December 28, 2016.

14. Ashraf, Malik Muhammad. "Balochistan and the Corridor." The News International. June 4, 2016.

15. Aziz, Shahid. "Putting Our Children in Line of Fire." The News International, January 6, 2013.

16. Constable, Pamela. "Missile Defense Plan Is Uniting US, India." The Washington Post.

17. May 20, 2001.

18. Hussain, Khurram. "CPEC Cost Build-Up." The Daily Dawn. December 15, 2016. Jinping, HE Xi. "Pak-China Dosti Zindabad." Daily Times, April 19 (2015).

19. Khan, Masood. "Pakistan-China Business Relations." Daily The Nation. April 17, 2012. Khan, Raza. "15,000 Troops of Special Security Division to Protect CPEC Projects." The

20. Daily Dawn, August 12, 2016.

21. Memon, Abdul Qadir. "Pak-China Trade: Importance of Negotiating the FTA." The Express Tribune, August 24, 2015.

22. Muhammad, Peer. "Pakistan Has Failed When It Comes to Trade with China." The Express Tribune, June 26, 2016.

23. Mustafa, Khalid. "Pakistan, China May Restart Talks on FTA-II." The News International, May 22, 2016.

24. Nagri, Jamil. "First Trade Activity Under CPEC Kicks Off." The Daily Dawn, November 1, 2016.

25. Paracha, Shahzad. "China and Pakistan Reluctant to Give Concessions in FTA II." Daily Times. December 1, 2016.

26. Perlez, Jane. "Rebuffed by China, Pakistan May Seek I.M.F. Aid." The New York Times, October 18, 2008.

27. Quinn, Ben. "Pakistan 'Gave China Access' to Downed US Helicopter." The Guardian, August 15, 2011.

28. Raja Asghar. "Nawaz Wants Common Agenda." Daily Dawn, June 6, 2013. Rana, Shahbaz. "ECC Approves Treaty to Protect Chinese Investors." The Express

29. Tribune, February 19, 2016.

30. Reddy, Muralidhar. "Dialogue on Sir Creek Begins." The Hindu. May 29, 2005. Rosenthal, Elisbeth. "U.S. Plane In China After It Collides With Chinese Jet." The New

31. York Times. April 2, 2001.

32. S, Arun. "Bilateral Trade Hit by Banks' Reluctance to Transact with Iran." Daily The Hindu. January 29, 2017.

33. Sharif, Nawaz. Times of India, May 28, 2006.

34. Zeb Khan, Mubarak. "CPEC Will Blaze a Trail." The Daily Dawn. August 30, 2016. Zulfqar, Saman. "CPEC: Future Prospects." The Daily Times, September 10, 2016.

35. "Pak-China Trade Increases by 18.2 Per cent." The Daily Dawn. April 27, 2016

36. Memon, Abdul Qadir. "Pak-China Trade: Importance of Negotiating the FTA." The Express Tribune, August 24, 2015.

37. Muhammad, Peer. "Pakistan Has Failed When It Comes to Trade with China." The Express Tribune, June 26, 2016.

38. Paracha, Shahzad. "China and Pakistan Reluctant to Give Concessions in FTA II." Daily Times. December 1, 2016.

39. Mirll, M. M. (2007). Vigorous Cold War Handshakes: Reviewing Nixon's 1972 China Trip. ProQuest.

40. Swaine, Michael D. "China: The Influence of History." The Diplomat, January 14, 2015

41. Cheema, Pervaiz Iqbal. "Significance of Pakistan-China Border Agreement of 1963."

42. Singh, Sarina. Pakistan and the Karakoram Highway.

43. Khalid Mustafa, "Pakistan, China May Restart Talks on FTA-II," The News International, May 22, 2016.

44. Perlez, Jane. "Rebuffed by China, Pakistan May Seek I.M.F. Aid." The New York Times, October 18, 2008.

45. "RAW Set Up Cell to Sabotage CPEC." The Express Tribune. April 14, 2016.

46. Jamil Nagri, "First Trade Activity Under CPEC Kicks Off," The Daily Dawn, November 1, 2016.

47. "Today Marks Dawn of New Era': CPEC Dreams Come True," The Daily Dawn, November 13, 2016.

48. "China Investing in Six Nuclear Projects in Pakistan." The Express Tribune, February 9, 2015.

49. Quinn, Ben. "Pakistan 'Gave China Access' to Downed US Helicopter." The Guardian, August 15, 2011'

50. "Press Conference at Dacca, 4 September 1965, SCMP, 3535. See also jen-minjih-pao commentary, 5 Septem"ber 1965.

51. "SCMP, 3336"

52. Malik Ayub Sumbal, "India and the Nuclear Suppliers Group (February 14, 2015)

53. Anwar Iqbal. "Formula for New NSG Members Leaves Pakistan out." Daily Dawn, December 28, 2016

54. Aziz, Shahid. "Putting Our Children in Line of Fire." The News International, January 6, 2013.

www.ingramcontent.com/pod-product-compliance
Lightning Source LLC
Chambersburg PA
CBHW062218150726
47991CB00006B/2333